MORAL DEVELOPMENT

MORAL DEVELOPMENT

A Guide to Piaget and Kohlberg

by
Ronald Duska
and
Mariellen Whelan

PAULIST PRESS
New York / Paramus / Toronto

Library of Congress
Catalog Card Number: 75-20863

ISBN: 0-8091-1892-0

Published by Paulist Press
Editorial Office: 1865 Broadway, N.Y., N.Y. 10023
Business Office: 400 Sette Drive, Paramus, N.J. 07652

Printed and bound in the
United States of America

Contents

ACKNOWLEDGMENTS

We wish to express our gratitude to Mr. Robert Heyer, managing editor of New Catholic World, for his encouragement and help with this work.

We also wish to thank Sister Ann Marie Durst, president of Rosemont College, and the faculty and staff of the college whose interest, cooperation and encouragement enabled us to produce this manuscript, as well as Mrs. Helen Whelan for her meticulous, thoughtful editing, and Mrs. Patricia Barr for her typing.

We are also grateful for the financial support from the Josephine C. Connelly Fund and for the cooperation of Sister Marcia Sichol and the faculty and students of the School of the Holy Child who were ever ready to respond to moral dilemmas.

We are grateful to those who have participated in our institutes and workshops for their enthusiasm for the subject and their penetrating questions which helped us to sharpen our thoughts on the important issues of moral development. Finally, we are grateful to Barbara Duska who contributed in numerous ways by keeping away distractions and encouraging one of the co-authors so that he could contribute his share of the work.

Introduction

What is a morally mature person? Many of us are inclined to think it is one who holds correct moral positions and acts in accord with such positions. In spite of a tendency to tolerance and pluralism, when it comes down to moral actions, many people find themselves commending some and disapproving others. We all have a system of values, and if we take these values seriously, we expect others to follow them and to agree with them. What is more, when faced with teaching such values, the natural tendency is to pass on what we know, or think we know, as correct positions.

If we do think there are some practices or actions that are correct and others that are wrong, if we think there are some objective do's and don'ts that are not simply determined by everybody making up his own mind, then do we not at least think that part of moral maturity is the knowledge of these do's and don'ts, rights and wrongs? Indeed, would not the complete picture of moral maturity involve not only the knowledge of the right or wrong, but also the character or will to act in accord with this straight thinking?

By and large, we are convinced that this structure of thinking about moral maturity is quite widespread in spite of the encroachment of situation ethics or the dissolution of absolutes about which we hear so much nowadays. There seems to be a little of that thinking in all of us, even if we do not like to admit it.

1

To the extent that such thinking has a practical application, it presents us with models for educating morally. If what needs to be accomplished is right thinking and straight acting, educating for moral maturity is simply plugging in the right answers to questions of "Would I?" or "Shouldn't I?" and then devising will-power exercises for the fortitude to follow the right path.

But let us examine this idea that moral maturity is knowing the right thing to do and doing it. Is it that simple? Anyone who has experienced a real moral dilemma, real moral anguish, knows that it is not so cut and dried. In the first place, even though we may be convinced that some actions are right or wrong in general, when we get down to particular cases with particular circumstances we often find that we are no longer so certain about the path to be followed. Further, we are also aware that someone can do the right thing for the wrong reasons. Is such a one morally mature, or are there mature and immature reasons?

Take an example of two girls, one fifteen and the other twenty-nine. The girl of fifteen gets invited to a high school prom. It is her first date with this escort, and after a lot of drinking he makes sexual advances. She answers "It's wrong" and refuses. The twenty-nine year old gets invited out by a salesman who came into the office, and after a number of drinks he asks her to go to his hotel room to make love. She refuses. Now, in both cases we have, first, a correct moral judgment and, second, the will to do what is right. Is that sufficient to indicate moral maturity in both cases? The answer is no, because an important factor has been left out— the *reason* for the moral judgment.

Let us continue our supposing for a moment. What if our fifteen year old is challenged by her boyfriend: "Why not?" Probably she would reply: "My mother told me it's wrong." But suppose our twenty-nine year old woman fended off her escort's passes with the same answer. Do we not find such a reason ludicrous coming from a supposedly mature woman? And although we might think our fifteen year old should have a better reason, are we not somewhat more patient with her than with the twenty-nine year old?

There are two points to the example. First, correct answers must be supplemented by substantial reasons if we are to label a moral judgment mature. Second, we expect more mature answers from more mature people, and we are willing to give the fifteen year old more time to grow up morally, at least with respect to her reasons. We expect older people to be more mature in their reasoning than younger people, since human beings develop moral maturity over a period of time.

It is apparent then that moral maturity demands morally mature reasons. A judgment that something is good may be considered correct, but it is only mature if it is formed by a mature reasoning process. But when is a reasoning process mature? Are there different processes? Can they be identified? Are there levels of maturity in reasoning about moral issues? How does one move through these levels? Is it a natural orderly process or is it haphazard? Can it be speeded up or slowed down? Once one recognizes that moral maturity depends on developing higher cognitive levels of reasoning these become important questions for those engaged in moral education. For if the goal of moral education is moral maturity, and if moral maturity is something that must be developed, then we should know about the developmental process and the ways of aiding its movement.

This book addresses the questions of development in moral judgment by presenting the work of two very important developmental psychologists who have studied the process of moral development, Jean Piaget and Lawrence Kohlberg. By concentrating their research on people's patterns of reasoning about moral decisions rather than on people's behavior, Piaget and Kohlberg have sketched a comprehensive picture of the way in which individuals develop morally. They have developed theories of moral development that show clearly what stages an individual goes through in achieving moral maturity.

It is an educational axiom that the most effective education takes place when one appeals to students at a level commensurate with their ability to learn. The theories of Piaget and Kohlberg identify such levels and detail procedures for determining which people occupy them. These theories, then, offer an invaluable pedagogic tool, but unfortunately knowledge of them is limited. Piaget's *The Moral Judgment of the Child* is a difficult and tedious work, while Kohlberg has not yet published a book in which he presents the essentials of his theory. Many of his articles can be found in *Collected Papers on Moral Development and Moral Education*, but at the moment this is available only through private sources. Both theorists have extremely important information for parents, educators and adults for their personal lives and their relationships with children and adolescents. It seems important then to present an exposition of the work of these men to the general reading public, and that is the task of this book.

The first two chapters deal with the theories of Piaget and Kohlberg. We have attempted to present their theories as faithfully as possible, while freeing the exposition from as much scientific or educational language as possible. Lacking the space to present all the voluminous research and data developed by the men and their followers, we have appealed to the reader's common sense intuitions and life experiences in order to support the plausibility of the theories and their stages. All this made it necessary that we have a coherent picture of our own as to how the various stages relate to one another. Such a picture may appear at some places in our own extrapolations. However, we are confident that such extrapolations do not do violence to, nor distort, the theories of Kohlberg and/or Piaget.

Moreover, we both approached the study of Piaget from our background as educators who are Christians. More specifically, we are Catholics. As is true with any religious tradition, within our tradition there has always been a strong emphasis on moral education. Thus it seemed desirable to present a chapter dealing with the relationship between moral developmental theory and Christian morality.

Finally, as educators, we are convinced that theories of development have important ramifications for educational theory and practice. Consequently, our last chapter deals with ways and means of utilizing what we learn from the theories in our educational dealings with others.

Needless to say, any information or explanations we have about man and his growth will be vitally important in helping men in their relationships with one another in our increasingly complex society. For too long the important findings of Piaget and Kohlberg have been overlooked or underexposed. It is our hope that this work will serve to give greater exposure to those findings.

I
Introduction to Developmental Theories

Any parent or teacher who has found himself saying to a child "How many times have I told you not to do that?" must wonder whether moral development is as painful to both adults and children as it sometimes appears to be. Assured that the child's hearing is fine, the adult is bewildered by the slowness of the child to assimilate principles and rules of right and wrong and perplexed about the means of assuring consistent application of those principles. Moral education has been equated with the teaching of rules and the development of character, which is expected to manifest itself in behavior that exemplifies the traditionally revered virtues of honesty, self-control, courage, friendliness and respect. The goal of most programs has been to instill these virtues so that they become internal principles guiding behavior and decision making. The means of accomplishing this is basically to confront the child repeatedly with examples of adults and older children who exhibit specific virtues by lecturing about these virtues, and by rewarding and punishing their practice or omission. This type of moral education differs little from teaching table manners and polite behavior.

Hartshorne and May of the University of Chicago conducted a long series of studies on stealing, cheating and lying that raised serious questions about such moral education programs in the home, schools, clubs and church groups. In every study they arrived at the same conclusions:

1. There is no correlation (relationship) between character training and actual behavior.

2. Moral behavior is not consistent in one person from one situation to another. A person who doesn't cheat in one situation may cheat in another. The circumstances are the most important factor.

3. There is no necessary relationship between what people say about morality and the way they act. People who express great disapproval of stealing and cheating may actually steal and cheat as much as everyone else.

4. Cheating is normally distributed around a level of moderate cheating—that is, normally everyone cheats a little.

These studies indicate that traditional forms of character or moral education are not effectively producing behavior that conforms to the principles being taught by the modeling, lecturing, rewarding and punishing. The implications of this study raise a serious question about moral development. Is there anything that parents and educators can do that will be effective?

A response to that question can be found in the work of two developmental psychologists, Jean Piaget and Lawrence Kohlberg, who have studied the process of growth in moral judgment. Their findings support the belief that moral judgment develops through a series of cognitive reorganizations called stages. Each stage has an identifiable shape, pattern and organization.

One of the clearest indications that such organizational shifts occur in a person's reasoning is the case of the young child who at one time judges the seriousness of an action solely on the basis of the size of the material consequences, but who at a later time judges not on the basis of the size of the consequences, but on the basis of the intention of the one performing the action.

That such different perspectives operate is clearly indicated by children's responses to the following dilemma:

A. A little girl named Marie wanted to give her mother a nice surprise and cut out a piece of sewing for her. But she didn't know how to use the scissors properly and cut a big hole in her dress.

B. A little girl named Margaret took her mother's scissors one day when her mother was out. She played with them for a while. Then, because she didn't know how to use them properly, she made a little hole in her dress.[1]

When asked which little girl should be punished more, two children answered in this way. Marilene, age 6: "The one who made the big hole." "Why?" "She made a big hole." Peter, age 7: "The second one." "Why?" "Well, the first one wanted to help her mother, and the second one was playing with the scissors and she shouldn't have been."

Marilene's response is typical of the stage where acts are judged by the size of the material consequences of the action. Peter, on the other hand, is able to perceive intention and is not distracted by the size of the hole in this instance, nor by the size of the material consequences in similar dilemmas.

Marilene is at a stage of development where she is not capable of judging an action in any way except by its material consequences.

No amount of explanation, lecturing, or even punishing would persuade Marilene that there is another way of looking at those two cases. There is in fact a wonderful inability to even entertain alternatives! Peter, though he at one time used the same criteria as Marilene in judging the degree of guilt, would be quite surprised at her reasoning, and would not remember that he had given similar responses at an earlier age.

This difference in responses is universal. Interview after interview with children repeatedly reinforces the fact that at certain stages things are seen from a perspective which is significantly different from an earlier or later perspective. Greater cognitive maturity, together with a variety of social experiences, will expand Marilene's perspective, at which time she will find her present way of judging right and wrong to be inadequate.

Moral development, then, is not a process of imprinting rules and virtues but a process involving transformation of cognitive structures. It is dependent on cognitive development and the stimulation of the social environment.

The Developmental Theory of Jean Piaget

Jean Piaget, currently co-director of the Institute of Educational Science in Geneva and professor of experimental psychology at the University of Geneva, has conducted research for more than forty years into the origins and development of cognitive structures and moral judgment in the early years of life. His studies on the moral judgment of the child were first published in 1932. Piaget analyzed children's verbal attitudes toward game rules, clumsiness, stealing and lying, and he explored many aspects of children's notions of justice. He identified two broad stages of development in the period between ages six to twelve. The youngest children are at a stage of heteronomy—that is, their rules are external laws which are sacred because they have been laid down by adults. Thus rules against damaging property, lying, or stealing are not seen as procedures established for the smooth functioning of the group or community, but are perceived as arbitrary rules, like "laws of the gods" which one must not transgress. This stage gradually diminishes in favor of autonomy where rules are seen to be the outcome of a free decision and worthy of respect in the measure that they have enlisted mutual consent. Then rules about property, lying and stealing are no longer obeyed because they were handed down by a superior, but they are seen as requirements for group relationships.[2]

We will look at Piaget's findings in each of the areas he explored to see the pattern of cognitive organization in the heteronomous stage and contrast that with the perspective of the autonomous stage. It is important to note here that autonomy for Piaget refers to freedom from the constraint of heteronomy. It is not the ultimate autonomy of the Kohlberg stages, but the basis for the social interaction that is necessary for moral development.

If, as Piaget believes, "all morality consists in a system of rules, and the essence of all morality is to be sought for in the respect which the individual acquires for those rules,"[3] then the crucial question for those interested in the development of morality is how the mind comes to respect rules. Piaget approached this question from two perspectives: first, consciousness of or respect for the rules, that is, the extent to which the rules act as a restraint; second, practice of the rules. Piaget was interested in finding out how much correspondence there is between the consciousness of or respect for the rules and the practice of them.

In order to study these two questions, Piaget selected a set of rules with which children of various ages would be familiar—the rules of the game of marbles. Like similar children's games, marbles is rarely formally taught, and generally the rules are learned without the influence of adult reward or punishment. Piaget observed children of different ages playing marbles and interrogated them about the rules—what they are, how they originated, and whether they could be changed. His main objective was to grasp the children's mental orientations toward rules in order to determine whether they believe in a heteronomy, that is, that the rules are external and sacred and cannot be changed by the players, or whether they are conscious of their own autonomy, that is, that the rules are the outcome of the mutual consent of the players. Piaget found several different orientations toward the rules of marbles in both consciousness of the rules and practice of them.

The youngest children, up to about age two, merely play with the marbles. No rules govern their activity; it is purely motor activity not guided by any intelligent goal. It may follow a pattern of repetition or motor rule, but there is in the child at this stage no consciousness of rules regulating the use of marbles. So we have at this stage, in regard to practice of the rules, merely motor activity, and a consciousness of the rules that is not coercive.

In the second stage, between the ages of two and six, the child observes older children playing marbles and he begins to imitate the ritual he observes. At this time, he is conscious that there are rules which govern this activity, and though his knowledge of them is rudimentary, he considers them sacred and untouchable. His practice of the rules is egocentric, that is, he is imitating what he has seen—the drawing of a circle, the positioning of the marbles, the aiming and shooting—for his own ends, unaware even of his isolation from the game as a social activity.

Let us expand a little on that. Unlike the child in the stage of motor activity, the two to six year old is conscious that rules regulate playing with marbles. However, he does not understand the game as a social activity. He has assimilated some parts of the social reality called marbles, but he is not yet capable of relating to others in an activity. He derives pleasure from the psychomotor activity of developing skills. At this stage, though children may have companions "playing" with them, each of them is in fact playing his own game, and if the companion is an adult, at the conclusion of the "game" the child is likely to say "Who won?" since he has no sense of how it all happens or of what winning means.

Cognitively the child in the egocentric stage has not yet differentiated himself from the external world. He doesn't know who he is, so he cannot place himself in a group as one of several others and mutually share an activity. However, there is a strong desire to imitate the ritual of the social group and to be associated with the society of those who play marbles. We will elaborate on this egocentric perspective later.

Egocentric play, then, is a transitional stage between the purely individualistic play of motor activity, where there was no awareness of what one ought to do with marbles, and the truly social play of cooperation.

The older children in the egocentric stage take an adamant verbal stand that the rules are sacred and unchangeable. They believe that the rules of marbles have been handed down from adults, and some even believe that God may have originally formulated them. Any alteration in the rules is considered a transgression.

The combination of the egocentric play and a belief in the sacredness of the rules is a curious paradox. On the one hand, the child feels the weight of obligation to honor and respect the rules regulating the game of marbles, while, on the other hand, he virtually ignores them when he plays. The resolution to the paradox is the child's perception of what he is doing, namely, that he is humbly submissive to each rule in every detail.

We see in this second stage heteronomous obedience. The child has a sense of obligation toward the rules, and they influence his actions, but he does not yet have the necessary cognitive structures to apply the rules in any form except imitation. Two children at this stage playing marbles will "do their own thing," each one oblivious to what the other is doing. We will see later what the consequences of this stage are for the practice of moral rules.

In the third stage, between the ages of seven and ten, the child moves from the purely psychomotor pleasure of the first two stages to pleasure gained from competing with others according to a set of rules that have been agreed to. The younger children in this stage are still influenced by a heteronomous obedience to the rules, but unlike the egocentric stage, the rules now are recognized as essential for regulating the game as a social activity. Children at this stage carefully watch each player to be sure he is playing by the rules agreed upon, because winning only has meaning in the context of a given set of rules.

Children at this stage do not understand the rules in all of their details. They will agree upon a set of rules for a particular game, but if they are questioned separately about those rules, one finds disagreement. However, the desire to cooperate with their peers is so strong that questionable practices are omitted and differences compromised. The result is a modified and simplified version of the game, but a true social activity.

During this stage there is a strong desire to understand rules and to play according to the rules that have been agreed upon. Gaps in intention and practice are more likely to be the result of a lack of knowledge of the rules rather than a lack of respect for those rules.

During the later ages of this period, heteronomy starts to give way to autonomy. It is through cooperative play, together with greater cognitive maturity, that the child sees rules as the product of mutual consent, rather than as a code of laws handed down by authorities.

Between the ages of eleven and twelve the child develops the ability for abstract reasoning, and at this time codification of the rules takes on great importance. Children at this age are interested in rules for rules' sake and frequently spend more time legislating for every possible event than they spend in actual play. Watch a group of eleven or twelve year old boys set up a baseball game on a new terrain. No detail will be left to chance; every tree and pebble that might affect the game in some way will be included in the frequently heated discussion setting up the rules. There is a strong desire to cooperate at this age, and the rules provide the structure for cooperation. It is at this stage, where rules are known very well and agreed upon in the minutest detail, that we find the closest correlation between consciousness of the rules and the practice of them. Tables I and II illustrate the development discerned by Piaget.

TABLE I. Stages in the Practice of Rules

Ages	0	1	2	3	4	5	6	7	8	9	10	11	12

Codification

Cooperation

Egocentric

Motor

TABLE II. Stages in Consciousness of Rules

Ages	0	1	2	3	4	5	6	7	8	9	10	11	12

Product of
    Mutual Consent

Sacred,
    Untouchable

Not Coercive

Let's look again at what Piaget found so that we may see how respect for rules develops. The young child up to about age seven or eight has an awesome respect for rules. They have a sort of mystical origin to him. He has not had adequate experiences in formulating rules to perceive them as anything but sacred and untouchable. This stage might be very appealing to some parents, except that the child's practice of the rules is very imperfect—not in his eyes, of course, but certainly in the objective order of things.

Respect for rules matures as the child reaches the stage where he is capable of cooperative activity and heteronomy begins to diminish. With the ascent of autonomy, respect for rules is seen in both the practice and the knowledge of them. Picture, if you will, the rules of marbles, or any game, being gradually assimilated as the child develops socially and cognitively from about age four to eleven or twelve, first in a purely imitative manner, then in simplified versions of the game, and finally to a point where the rules are generalized and codified, and you see the process of development of respect for rules.

Not all rules are submitted to this type of critical examination by the eleven and twelve year old, nor even by adults. Some motor rules simply become habits, and in every person's life there are areas of heteronomous submission—for example, unquestioning submission to a doctor's orders or to Church rules or to state and federal laws. Heteronomy and autonomy describe the process of development rather than the total mental orientation of the individual. One can be autonomous in his practice of some rules, heteronomous in his knowledge and practice of other rules. In fact, Piaget points out that heteronomy is the unifying factor in some adult societies and organizations. These are social groups who are persuaded that they have the truth and who see their task to be one of imprinting that truth, those beliefs and norms, on succeeding generations.

There are several important points to be noted in Piaget's study of the development of respect for rules. *First,* it is through cooperative activity that the child develops an understanding of the purpose and origin of rules. As the child begins to relate to his peers in cooperative play, he experiences relationships of mutual respect. He sees his opponent as someone like himself, and he experiences the other's respect for him. Prior to this, the only respect the child knew was unilateral, that is, the respect he had for adult authority. Because the adult is both bigger and more powerful, the child does not experience mutuality in that relationship. The adult controls; he can give or withhold, punish or reward. The child has no sense of equality with the adult. It is this relationship of unilateral respect or adult constraint that perpetuates the stage of heteronomy. Rules are seen as emanating from adults and enforced by them, and the child's relationship toward adults is one of respect, so he obeys.

In the peer relationships, the element of unilateral respect is absent, and the children meet together as equals. This provides the social environment for cooperative play, for constructing rules through mutual consent, and for developing autonomy.

Some other important points to be noted are: *second,* children through age seven or eight consider themselves humbly submissive to all of the rules that govern their lives; *third*, the heteronomous child, while holding a divine respect for rules, does not have adequate understanding or motivation to be consistent in the practice of rules; *fourth*, not until a child is at the level of autonomy in a given rule or set of rules will his knowledge and respect approximate his practice of the rules.

Some implications can be drawn from these findings to aid parents and educators in their work with children. First, the goal and direction of the development of respect for rules is an autonomous understanding and practicing of them. To achieve autonomy the child must move out of the stage of heteronomy. The means of achieving this is through cooperative activities in relationships of mutual respect, that is, in activities where there is not an authority-subject relationship—for example, classroom group projects where the children plan the goals and debate and argue among themselves how to achieve the goals and how to divide the work equally. This is difficult to achieve in the adult-child relationship with young children because of their natural bent toward unilateral respect. However, several principles seem worthy of mention as guidelines.

The use of adult superior force and commands demanding a blind obedience reinforce the unilateral, heteronomous view of rules, whereas dialogue and discussions that bring about mutual understanding and agreement lead to cooperation, and eventually to autonomy.

This could have practical applications in formulating rules for the good order of the home or classroom. Even when the necessary cognitive development for true social activities is not present, it is more helpful for the child to participate in the formulation of rules than to have them pronounced by adults for his submission.

Efforts to help the child understand the effects of his actions on the family community or classroom community will facilitate the development of mutual respect and cooperation. These lead to greater autonomy in the practice and understanding of rules.

From about age six or seven, opportunities for peer cooperative activity will facilitate development of mutual respect and movement out of egocentric thought and heteronomous obedience.

Classrooms that provide ample opportunities for the children to work together are a good means of assuring this.

Heteronomy and the Child's Judgment of Right and Wrong

Let us turn our attention now to the influence of heteronomy on the child's judgment of right and wrong. All rules are similar to the young child, so the process of developing respect for moral rules will be identical to that of game rules, and there will be a period where moral rules are seen as sacred and untouchable, and where the practice of them is egocentric, that is, merely an imitation of what has been observed. Piaget called this period in understanding of moral rules the period of *moral realism*, which he defines as "the tendency to regard duty and the value attaching to it as self-subsistent and independent of the mind, as imposing itself regardless of the circumstances in which the individual finds himself."[4] Duty for the child of this age is spelled out in the commands and rules of adults, and these are seen to be a good in themselves simply because they emanate from adults. Thus, any act that shows obedience to adults or to rules is good, and likewise any act that does not conform to rules is bad. Duty, then, is heteronomous obedience. The rules are taken literally, according to the letter of the law, and acts are interpreted in terms of their exact conformity to the letter of the law. For this age child, rules are exacting in their demands, and there are no extenuating circumstances that modify the application of the letter of the rule.

Thus Marilene, the six year old referred to earlier, interprets the two acts of cutting which resulted in material damage exactly in terms of the letter of the law of material damage. One can sense her reasoning—it is wrong to cut holes in fabric or clothing. In this instance, then, the fabric with the bigger hole breaks the rule more; therefore, that child who cuts the bigger hole should be punished more.

Let's see whether we can put ourselves in the cognitive perspective of the heteronomous, egocentric child. In the first place the egocentric child is surrounded by rules that regulate almost every aspect of his life, and unlike the very young child, the egocentric child feels a sense of obligation toward the rules. This sense of obligation arises when a child accepts commands from adults he respects, such as commands not to lie or not to steal. It is the beginning of a moral conscience. This may seem very positive and attractive to adults looking for docility from the young, but we shall see that there are severe intellectual handicaps for the egocentric child which influence his ability to respond to those commands.

Let us take another look at the cognitive aspects of egocentricity and elaborate on the child's inability to differentiate himself from his environment, that is, from the people and events around him. Piaget describes cognitive egocentrism as a state when the organism is unaffected by contact with reality. That is, he cannot assimilate his environment to his thought processes because he does not yet have the cognitive structures to sort out events, people and ideas. He confuses external and internal. His dreams, wishes and inner thoughts are as real for him as chairs, tables and sofas. Cognitively he has no ability to distinguish facts from dream occurrences, true information from false opinions. He accepts everything he hears or sees uncritically without distinguishing the real from the fantastic. He cannot distinguish between past and present. Something told to him in the present, he may confuse and think he has known always. He does not see his viewpoint as one of many possible others. He feels no compunction to justify his reasons to others, or to look for possible contradictions in his logic.

If you can mentally place yourself in a situation where you are in a group that is discussing a topic in your language, but in an area of very complex subject matter foreign to you, you have the cognitive set of the egocentric child. He has the tools to speak and to hear the language, but he cannot absorb all that is spoken to him and all that happens around him.

Because he has virtually no sense of who he is as a person and what he personally wants, other children and adults have almost limitless power over him. He yields to their every suggestion and wish and accepts them without knowing that he does. From the point of view of action, he interprets in his own fashion what he has observed, believing that he is imitating perfectly.

Now, what are the implications of egocentricity for moral judgment? Just this: the egocentric child who does not yet know himself finds his identity in submission to adult rules. He is not yet capable of the social intercourse of cooperation, so he finds pleasure in a feeling of continuous communion between himself and the world of the elders. This communion is his unilateral respect for fidelity to the letter of their rules. However, his understanding of those rules is filtered through his own cognitive limitations. We will find in moral rules, as we did in rules of a game, that the egocentric child's intention is to submit to the rules laid down, but these, like many other experiences, remain external to his conscience and do not become internalized rules directing his behavior.

In order to examine the effects of moral realism on the child's judgment, Piaget focused on the issues of clumsiness, stealing and lying. He constructed stories about each issue that forced the child to make a judgment about behavior that deviated from the rules against breaking or damaging property, stealing and lying. We shall examine his findings on each of these issues to see the effects of heteronomy and moral realism.

Clumsiness plays an important role in the child's life, and regardless of how an act of clumsiness occurs, it is usually associated in the child's mind with adult anger. Stories were devised to provoke the child to compare two kinds of clumsiness—one the consequences of a well-intentioned act, but involving considerable material damage, the other the consequence of an ill-intentioned act, but involving little material damage. Children were interviewed individually, told a set of stories, asked to repeat them to determine whether the stories were understood, and then asked whether the children in the stories were equally guilty, or which child was the naughtier, and why. Besides the set of stories of Marie and Margaret with the scissors, Piaget used these other sets of stories.[5]

I. A. A little boy named John is in his room. He is called to dinner. He goes into the dining room. But behind the door there is a chair, and on the chair there is a tray with fifteen cups on it. John couldn't have known that all this was behind the door. He goes in, the door knocks against the tray, bang go the fifteen cups, and they all get broken!

B. Once there was a little boy whose name was Henry. One day when his mother was out he tried to get some jam out of the cupboard. He climbed up onto a chair but he couldn't reach it. However, while he was trying to get it he knocked over a cup. The cup fell down and broke.

II. A. There was a little boy named Julian. His father had gone out and Julian thought it would be fun to play with his father's inkwell. First he played with the pen and then he made a little blot on the tablecloth.

B. A little boy named Augustus once noticed that his father's inkwell was empty. One day, when his father was away, he decided to fill the inkwell in order to help his father, so that he would find it full when he came home. But while he was opening the ink bottle, he made a big blot on the tablecloth.

The younger children, up to about age eight, judged guilt on the basis of the size of the material damage, that is, on the basis of objective responsibility. These children responded as Marilene did, consistently applying the letter of the law. The naughtier child is John "because he broke fifteen cups," Augustus "because he made a big spot," and Marie "because she cut a big hole." Peter, age seven, responds to the cup story that John is the naughtier "because he knocked down more things." (This is the same Peter quoted earlier. Peter is a good example of a seven year old who is moving from heteronomy to autonomy. The cup story was the only instance where Peter made his judgment on the basis of size of damage rather than on the basis of intention.) From these children's responses we get some perception of the egocentric child's interpretations of rules on the issue of property damage and breakage. Because a child of this age cannot identify with others or relate to them, there is no consideration given to the *intention* of the children involved in the breakage. This way of judging on the basis of objective responsibility, that is, on the basis of the size of damage and by the letter of the law without concern for the intentions, diminishes as the child grows older. Piaget found no instances of moral realism in clumsiness after age ten, and he found the average age for judgment on the basis of objective responsibility to be age seven.

Stealing stories were constructed to provoke the child to compare selfishly motivated acts of stealing with those that are well intentioned. The aim again was to determine whether the child pays more attention to motive or to material results. The same questions were asked: Are these children equally guilty, which of the two is naughtier, and why? These are the stories.[6]

IV. A. Alfred meets a friend who is very poor. This friend tells him that he has had no dinner that day because there was nothing to eat in his home. Then Alfred goes into a baker's shop, and since he has no money, he waits until the baker's back is turned and steals a roll. Then he runs out and gives the roll to his friend.

B. Henriette goes into a shop. She sees a pretty piece of ribbon on a table and thinks to herself that it would look very nice on her dress. So, while the saleslady's back is turned, she steals the ribbon and runs away at once.

V. A. Albertine had a little friend who kept a bird in a cage. Albertine thought the bird was very unhappy, and she was always asking her friend to let him out, but the friend wouldn't. So one day when her friend wasn't there, Albertine stole the bird. She let it fly away and hid the cage in the attic so that the bird would never be shut up in it again.

B. Juliet stole some candy from her mother one day when her mother was not there. She hid and ate them.

Children up to about age seven evaluate these stories on the basis of objective responsibility, that is, the material result, independent of the motive. Marilene, age six, says Alfred is naughtier in the first pair of stories, "because, well, a roll costs about twelve cents and, well, a ribbon costs less." Likewise, Albertine is naughtier because she stole a cage, and a piece of candy costs less. Once again, intention is not a consideration for judgment. The size of the material consequences of any act is the universal criterion of judgment for the child in the stage of moral realism. Beyond the age of seven, Piaget found no instances of judging by objective responsibility in the stealing stories. Children after that age compared the intentions of the actors in the stories and judged Alfred and Albertine, the well-intentioned actors, as less naughty than Henriette and Juliet.

The clumsiness and stealing stories reveal two distinct stages in moral judgment—the stage of heteronomy and moral realism where acts are judged on the basis of objective responsibility, and the stage where acts are judged on the basis of subjective responsibility. It is clear that judgment on objective responsibility is the product of the immature mind acting under adult constraint. Adults have educated the child implicitly or explicitly to a rudimentary knowledge of right and wrong. The child's immature mind, together with his heteronomous respect, allows him to interpret and apply these rules literally.

How does the ability to judge by subjective responsibility develop? Subjective responsibility is as much the product of cooperation as objective responsibility is the product of constraint. When the child has the cognitive and social maturity to diminish the force of heteronomous respect, he is also able to take the role of others and see actions from perspectives other than his own—therefore, to judge by subjective responsibility. Cooperative peer activity is a strong influence in facilitating that process, because heteronomy and unilateral respect are absent from such relationships. It is in these relationships that egocentrism diminishes and true social intercourse becomes a reality.

Lying is a much more serious problem area for children. It is a natural tendency for young children, and appears to be tied to egocentric thought. The child cannot distinguish his own private dreams, wishes and imaginings from what actually exists. His inner life is as real to him as the physical world. He is confronted, however, with adult admonitions not to lie. He is frequently told by older siblings and parents that "that isn't true," "you did not do that," "you're lying; I'm going to tell Mother." Here is the true clash of egocentric thought and adult constraint. What does the child make of this?

Piaget examined the question of lying from several perspectives. He was interested in how children define a lie, what criteria they apply to determine how bad a lie is, and the reasons why people shouldn't lie.

Piaget found a developmental scheme in children's definitions of a lie which is illustrated in Table III.

TABLE III. Definitions of a Lie

Age	0	1	2	3	4	5	6	7	8	9	10	11	12
Any statement intentionally false											▬	▬	▬
Something that isn't true									▬	▬	▬		
Something that isn't true including mistakes							▬	▬	▬				
A naughty word				▬	▬	▬							

     Up to about age six or seven, a lie is a naughty word. It is a verbal performance to which adults react negatively. The child interprets lying, a verbal utterance, as being in the category of obscenities and other language the family finds objectionable. This is his egocentric interpretation of the rule. As we have seen, the child at this age confuses myth and reality, and he cannot relate to others meaningfully, so he has no experience of the effect of lying; hence he associates it with other verbal rules and calls it a naughty word.

     Between the ages of six and ten the child defines a lie as something that isn't true. Mistakes, exaggerations, anything that isn't a fact—all these are considered to be lies. Two plus two equals five, though identified as a mistake, is also called a lie. About the age of eight, while lies are still defined as something that is not true, mistakes are no longer considered to be lies. In both of these definitions—that is, a lie is something that is not true, including mistakes, and a lie is only something that is not true—there is a lingering heteronomy. These children have not yet made the rule their own.

     It is between the ages of eight and ten, when the child has a strong desire to cooperate, that he experiences a need for truth in his various expanded relationships of mutual respect. Thus, at age ten, the definition of a lie is "any statement that is intentionally false." The child moves away from moral realism, where he judged lying by objective responsibility—that is, if it's not true, it's a lie—to judging by intention. This perspective cannot be imprinted on the child by lecturing or by punishing. It is through experiences of cooperative living in the various communities of which the child is part that he develops an understanding of lying as a violation of community trust.

Moral realism in children's definitions of lies probably lingers longer than realism in clumsiness and stealing for a variety of reasons. First, lying is natural to the child; he has no felt need for truth, just as young children playing with marbles have no felt need for mutual understanding. Second, adults may punish lying more severely than other faults because they think it is important to impress on the child the heinousness of lying. If that is the case, heteronomy in regard to lying will be more difficult to overcome. Third, the child cannot understand the fault in lying until he is in a society of mutual cooperation and experiences the need for truth. Hence, it remains a heteronomous rule to which to submit until about age ten.

Piaget next examined how a child judges the content of a lie and the consequences of a lie. In order to separate content from consequences, stories were constructed first that include lies resulting in no material consequences. These stories enabled Piaget to assess what constituted bigness in a lie itself apart from the distraction of some measurable consequences. The child was provoked to compare the content of the lies and asked which actor was naughtier and why. Here are the stories that were used.[7]

I. A. A little boy goes for a walk in the street and meets a big dog who frightens him very much. He goes home and tells his mother he has seen a dog that was as big as a cow.

B. A child comes home from school and tells his mother that the teacher has given him good marks, but it is not true; the teacher has given him no marks at all, either good or bad. His mother was very pleased and rewards him.

II. A. A boy was playing in his room. His mother called and asked him to deliver a message for her. He didn't feel like going out, so he told his mother that his feet were hurting. But it wasn't true. His feet weren't hurting him in the least.

B. A boy wanted very much to go for a ride in a car, but no one ever asked him. One day he saw a man driving a beautiful car. When he got home he told his parents that the gentleman in the car had stopped and had taken him for a little drive. But it was not true; he had made it all up.

III. A. A boy couldn't draw very well, but he would have liked very much to be able to draw. One day he was looking at a beautiful drawing that another boy had done, and he said: "I made that drawing."

B. A boy was playing with the scissors one day when his mother was out and he lost them. When his mother came in he said that he hadn't seen them and hadn't touched them.

The results are interesting. In the case of the stories on clumsiness and stealing the younger children judged actions on the basis of the size of the material consequences, regardless of the actor's intentions. The same tendency was apparent in the children's judgment of these three stories, but the material aspects are less obvious. The young children judged guilt on the basis of the "size" of the lie, that is, the farther it was from the truth, the bigger the lie was and the naughtier the liar. What in later development will be called an exaggeration, at this stage is a more serious offense than a lie closer to the truth, which, if it is believed, is only a little lie, or no lie at all. Thus, in the first story, the boy who says he has seen a dog as big as a cow is naughtier than the boy who told his mother he had good marks because "there aren't any dogs as big as cows," "no one would believe him," "it's a bigger lie." Similarly, the boy who said he had gone for a ride is naughtier than the boy who said his feet hurt, because "gentlemen don't stop and take children for rides," "it's a bigger lie," "his mother would know he hadn't gone for a ride." The boy who claimed to have done the drawing is naughtier because "no one would believe him," "he didn't know how to draw and he said he did it." The children agree in all three stories that both lies in each set of stories do indeed deceive, but the children judge the seriousness of the lie strictly on the degree of likelihood.

These judgments once again point to the distortion in the moral judgments of the child in the stage of moral realism. We see again in the younger children the effects of egocentric thought. A lie is something that is not true, so the more untrue it is, the worse it is. Piaget found age seven to be the average age for judging objectively by the size of the lie, and age ten the average age for judging subjectively. By age ten the children judge by intention, and they apply the opposite criteria to the content. It is also at this age that a lie is defined in terms of intention. At this age, the less a lie appears to be one, that is, the closer it is to the truth, the more serious it is, because it may be believed. The farther a lie is from the truth, the less serious it is because no one will believe it.

Stories were then constructed to provoke the child to compare actors' intentions with and without material consequences. In these stories Piaget was trying to assess how children measured responsibility for lying. In one story the actor makes a simple mistake, but it leads to harmful consequences; in the other story the actor deliberately deceives, but the consequences are negligible. Here are the stories.[8]

> IV. A. A child who didn't know the names of streets very well was not quite sure where Main Street was. One day a gentleman stopped him in the street and asked where Main Street was. So the boy answered, "I think it is that way." But it was not. The gentleman completely lost his way and could not find the house he was looking for.
>
> B. A boy knew the names of the streets quite well. One day a gentleman asked him where Main Street was. But the boy wanted to play a trick on him, and he said; "It's there." He showed him the wrong street, but the gentleman didn't get lost and managed to find his way again.

The results were similar to the stories of clumsiness and stealing. Children up to about age seven think only of the material consequences and respond that the boy who didn't know where Main Street was was naughtier because the man got lost. Even though the boy's action is identified as a mistake, he nevertheless is the naughtier. The second boy didn't make the man lose his way, so he shouldn't be punished at all. By age nine children judge these stories by intention, and then the boy who deliberately deceived is the one who should be punished, and the one who made a mistake should not be punished, because he made a mistake.

Children's responses to the query "Why must we not tell lies?" provide further insight to the reasoning structures of the child. Up to age six, a lie is wrong because it is punished. If lies weren't punished, it would be perfectly all right to tell them. There is no understanding of mutuality or of reciprocity in relationships. Lies are forbidden—one more of those rules from adults or from God. At a more advanced stage a lie is a fault in itself, even if it is not punished. The rule now has become obligatory, but nevertheless remains heteronomous, external to the child's mind and conscience. When unilateral respect has yielded to mutual respect, at about age ten, children then say a lie is wrong because it is in conflict with mutual trust.

As we might have predicted, a complementary progression in understanding why lies are wrong can be seen in the responses to the query "Is it just the same to tell lies to grown-ups and to children?" The younger children say lies between children are allowed because "grown-ups are bigger," "it doesn't matter to a child," "a child can't tell whether it's a lie." Once again the child responds from a heteronomous obedience. Rules are made by adults and enforced by adults, and at this stage no rules govern relationships among peers. Respect is completely unilateral from child to adult. Gradually the attitude changes, and then to deceive one's colleagues is as bad or even worse than to deceive adults.

The explorations of children's ideas about lying reveal—even more clearly than their ideas of clumsiness and stealing—the slow pace of development in their understanding, the serious distortions in their perceptions of moral rules, the fact of a stage of *moral realism*, and the dangers of interpreting the child's compliance to rules as comprehension and acceptance of them. A moral education program in the family or school is short-sighted if its goal is compliance to rules. From the children's responses to the definition of a lie, and in their responses to why a lie is wrong, it is clear that young children see a rule as something tacked onto their consciousness, as some parameter outside them that acts as a restraining force. The rule against lying is not a self-chosen principle guiding decisions until the child has had adequate social experiences to comprehend the need for truth. It is clear that neither punishments nor reprimands will facilitate what is essentially a socializing process. The inconsistency in application of the rule which Hartshorne and May found is understandable when one reflects on the child's understanding of what *the rule* is. Setting rule compliance as a moral goal actually *hinders* moral development because such an approach reinforces and prolongs the period of moral realism, where the child is not subjecting rules to the critical examination necessary to gain autonomy.

What can be done to facilitate development from heteronomy to autonomy in moral rules? Heteronomy diminishes as the child experiences societies of mutual respect. This is difficult to create in the family because of the superior-inferior relationships that naturally exist and elicit from the child a unilateral respect. Emphasis should be put on the family as a cooperative group, mutually setting up rules for the good order of everybody in the house, and mutually concerned and affected by the violations of those rules. Milk spilled at the table through carelessness by a child frequently provokes a more aggravated response from adults than the same careless act caused by an adult. It is important for adults to stress their obligations and deficiencies. To sit quietly with a child and discuss the effects on the family of some irresponsible action on his part stimulates the empathy that is essential to the development of mutual respect and, as we will see later, essential to development to the higher levels of moral judgment that Kohlberg describes.

The child needs help to judge actions by intentions. This is a perspective that he simply does not have in early years. Both family and school have ample opportunities to provide this in discussing stories, in judging other people's actions, and in reflecting on the child's actions. A child's often uttered statement "I didn't mean to do it" indicates that he is beginning to look at actions by intention, and if the societies of family and school appear not to consider intentions, but only consequences, the child may rebel. We saw in the rules of the game of marbles that about age eight to ten the child has a strong desire to cooperate. Piaget believes that if at this age a child finds a society that develops mutual trust and cooperation, a new type of morality will emerge, one of reciprocity, in place of heteronomous obedience.

The Development of Justice

We began our study of moral development with Piaget's quote that the essence of all morality is in the respect one holds for the rules. We have seen in our study of clumsiness, stealing and lying that there are two kinds of respect and hence two moralities. Unilateral respect develops a morality of heteronomy, while mutual respect develops a morality of autonomy. We have spent some time familiarizing ourselves with the first type, morality of heteronomy or constraint. We will now examine more closely the morality that develops through cooperation, and specifically the concept of justice which seems to be a direct result of cooperation. Piaget believes that "the sense of justice, though naturally capable of being reinforced by the precepts and example of the adult, is largely independent of these influences, and requires nothing more for its development than the mutual respect and solidarity which holds among children themselves."[9] He contrasts the rule of justice to adult rules which have been imposed on the child and says: "The rule of justice is a sort of immanent condition of social relationships or a law governing their equilibrium, and as the solidarity among children grows we shall find this notion of justice gradually emerging in almost complete autonomy."

From our earlier studies we can predict that the egocentric, heteronomous child's notions of justice will be related to duty toward adult authority. Their focus will be on retributive justice, which is defined by due proportion between acts and punishments. As mutual respect and solidarity become more influential in the child's life, retributive justice will become less important than distributive justice, which is defined by equality.

(a) *Retributive Justice.* Let's look first at notions of retributive justice. We have seen in the previous sections how distorted are children's perceptions of right and wrong. We have also seen that wrong is pretty much defined in terms of what is punished, and that the child's strong attachment to unilateral respect interferes with the process of comprehending the rules and making them his own. Yet he has a strong tendency to be submissive to them and he regards them as a good in their own right. Breaking the rules arouses the anger of the adults he respects and interferes with his relationship with them which is his only attachment to society. He naturally then seeks some means of appeasing the anger and restoring the communion with his elders. Punishment is the means, and the more severe the better. If given several punishments to select, he will base his selection on the criteria of what hurts the most, not what is related to the offense. Thus, sending a child to his room for breaking a toy, depriving him of some pleasure for not eating his supper, and requiring him to copy a poem several times for talking in class are all considered by the young child as fair punishments because they are things the child would not like to do. He believes that a child punished in this manner is less likely to commit the fault again, as contrasted with a child who is not punished, but merely verbally admonished. Most parents could present cold statistical evidence that would contradict the young child's notion of how efficacious punishment is, but this belief in expiatory punishment seems to go hand in hand with heteronomous obedience and a morality of constraint. Rules are seen as a kind of mystical taboo that requires expiation when violated.

Between the ages of eight and twelve when cooperation and mutual respect are developing, notions of expiatory punishment diminish in favor of punishments that restore the social bond, that is, punishments by reciprocity. Fair punishments then are those that are related to the offense, either by making the offender suffer the material consequences of his act or omission, or by doing to the offender something comparable to what he has done. Sheer chastisement is not considered fair by the older children. They do not choose the punishments that hurt the most, but the ones that relate to the offence committed.

They now participate in social relationships as members of

various communities. There is an understanding of the need for rules and regulations to govern those communities. The child is also able at this age to put himself in the place of others and see the effects of rule violations. Piaget has classified punishments by reciprocity that are considered fair by the older children:

1. Exclusion—momentary or permanent from the social group itself.
2. Suffering the immediate and material consequences of the act.
3. Depriving of the thing misused.
4. Doing to the offender exactly what he has done.
5. Restitutive punishment—paying for or restoring what was damaged.
6. Censure only—with no punishment—concerned only to make the transgressor realize how he has broken the bond of solidarity.

It seems important to remember that the child at this age tends toward cooperation and mutual respect. Whatever punishments are imposed should be ones that are aimed at furthering the child's education in responsible, cooperative living. It seems equally important to protect the young child from his focus on expiation and the necessity for punishment. Although the young child will interpret even punishments intended for reciprocity as expiation, it seems important to educate him toward the goal of punishment as a means of restoring the bond of solidarity.

(b) *Group Responsibility.* Piaget explored another aspect of interest to parents and to teachers, and that is the notion of group responsibility. Every teacher has resorted to threatening, if not actually implementing the threat, to retain the class after school until "the guilty one" confesses. I recall one Halloween that our house was enveloped in darkness, uninviting to masked trick and treaters from outside and confining to four disappointed trick and treaters inside, in punishment for the misbehavior of one or two of us. I also recall a family cancelling its Bermuda spring vacation for its seven members, because two of the children did not receive good grades on their report cards.

How do children view group punishment? Do they see responsibility as communicable?

Piaget devised three different situations where adults resorted to group punishment. In the first instance a mother goes out, leaving all of her children playing together. When she returns she finds that one of them has been disruptive. The guilty child makes no effort to conceal his identity, but nevertheless the mother punishes all of the children. Children of all ages considered that type of group punishment unfair, even young children whose strong ties of unilateral respect usually distort their judgment in favor of the adult.

The other two types of situations involved, first, an instance where the group knows the identity of the offender but will not tell the adult, and, second, an instance where the group knows the offender is one of the group, but his identity is unknown to the group and the offender does not own up to the crime. In these instances the younger children believe group punishment is fair, for two reasons. First, young children have a strong belief in the necessity for punishment for an act that violates a rule. So it is fair for a teacher or parent to punish the group if someone has offended. The moral law of these children consists solely of rules imposed by adults. Therefore, if one of these rules is broken, the adult will naturally be angry, and this anger will take the form of some kind of punishment. If there is no single individual to receive the punishment, then the whole group must take it. Second, in the instance where the children know who the perpetrator is but will not tell the adult, the younger children, because of their unilateral respect, believe concealment of information from adults is wrong, so each member of the group deserves punishment for not telling. For that reason group punishment is fair.

The older children judge the two instances differently and on the basis of solidarity. In the case where the offender is known to the group, but the group has chosen not to reveal his identity to the adult, the older children recognize that they have opted for group solidarity against adult authority and that in this instance group punishment is fair. The group feels it has freely chosen to accept responsibility for one member's actions. When the group does not know which of its members is guilty, though, it does not feel that it freely unites to protect that member, and a group punishment in this instance is considered unfair by the older children.

I had occasion to ask a group of college students once whether they could recall any collective punishment that had been imposed on them in their school years, and whether they could remember whether they considered the punishment fair at that time. One student recalled an instance in a fifth grade class that exemplifies the kind of group solidarity that is prepared to accept the consequences of a member's actions, but that can also test any adult. The teacher was described as a prissy, old maidish type, who always dressed in long black skirts. On this particular occasion one of the boys chalked up the teacher's chair before she arrived. Sometime later in the morning the teacher discovered chalk dust all over her long black skirt. (Now comes the crucial moment in any teaching career.) This teacher retreated to the cloakroom, where she removed her long, black, chalky skirt, wrapped herself in one of the boy's mackinaws, and thrust the skirt out the door of the cloakroom, announcing to the class (now solidly united in all the worst aspects of cooperative activity) that she would not emerge from the cloakroom until the skirt was taken to the cleaners and returned spotless. Some debate over advantages and disadvantages of the ultimatum must have ensued at this moment, but the student's recollection was that everybody chipped in money and the skirt was rushed out to the cleaners. I do not know whether this teacher had read Piaget or not, but she gambled that there was just enough vestige of heteronomy in the children's attitudes toward authority to enable her to threaten a withdrawal. Such is moral development that a group two years older might have responded differently!

It occurs to me that questions of group responsibility have interesting implications for religious development. Traditionally, mankind's present condition has been explained by Adam's fall. How do children view this in terms of justice? In their eyes is the group being unjustly punished for the sin of one of its members? Conversely, how do they interpret Christ's action of assuming the guilt for all of us in his death on the cross? It would seem that the solidarity of mankind is a fairly obscure notion for children to grasp while they are still growing into an understanding of solidarity in their own family units.

(c) *Immanent Justice.* Young children believe that all nature is in a partnership conspiring to maintain the universal order and punishing children's lack of conformity to that order. This is clearly seen in the child's belief in an immanent justice, which Piaget describes as automatic punishments emanating from things themselves.[10] If a young child has done something wrong, or hears of another child who has offended rules in some way, he is not surprised—in fact he almost expects—to be punished by some fortuitous event, like having the sidewalk trip him, causing him to scrape his knee, or having a dog chase and frighten him. If asked why these events occurred, a child will answer that it is because a rule was broken and the child is being punished. This strong belief in immanent justice seems to have two causes: one stems from the role of punishment in the child's life, and the other from a belief in a purposeful order in the actions of animate and inanimate objects. Adults have made punishment synonomous with rule breaking. Punishment is both the means of defining wrongdoing and the expected condition following wrongdoing. This condition, combined with the child's inability to dissociate physical and biological laws from adult-made laws, creates an environment that for the child appears to have unity of purpose in regard to wrongdoing. The dog might not know that the child stole an apple, but there is some power that urged the dog to punish the child. This belief in immanent justice is frequently reinforced by adult comments like: "Let that be a punishment to you" or "That serves you right for hitting your sister." God also is brought into the picture to add to the child's mystical beliefs: "I told you God would punish you for that" and "See, God's punishing you." In these instances, adults are taking advantage of a child's chance misfortune and reinforcing the child's belief in immanent justice.

About age eight the child begins to dissociate physical, biological and human laws from adult laws and powers, and the belief in immanent justice diminishes. Piaget believes there are other factors that lead the child away from a belief in immanent justice, one of which is the moral experience that leads the child to discover the imperfection of adult justice. "When, as is almost bound to happen, a child is submitted to unjust treatment by his parents or his teachers, he will be less inclined to believe in a universal and automatic justice."[11]

(d) *Distributive Justice.* One of the positive aspects of the child's development away from adult constraint is the expansion of his perspective and his expression of sensitivity to the human factors involved in a given situation. The young child is confined in his assessment of right and wrong to a fairly black and white decision. If someone has been disobedient, punish him; if someone has broken cups, punish him; if someone has inadvertently cut a hole in a piece of fabric, punish him. The broader perspective and sensitivity of the older children to the context of the situation is clearly seen when situations involving retributive justice, that is, expiation for a fault committed, are posed with situations involving distributive justice, that is, equality of treatment in the manner in which things are divided and distributed.

When faced with a situation of a mother whose preference for an obedient daughter over a disobedient daughter is manifest on a particular occasion in her distribution of pieces of cake, the larger piece going to the obedient daughter, the young children consider the mother's action a fair one. Disobedience should be punished and obedience should be rewarded. The young children focus on expiation for evil, not equality in distribution. Older children show much greater sensitivity to various factors in the content of the act and in the possible consequences. For them the act is unfair: things should be distributed equally, and the mother should love both daughters equally and be kind to both. If the mother gives one girl a small piece, she may become worse and not try to be obedient.

The turning point in weighing equality against retribution is about age nine. It is interesting to note, as we saw in the last section, that older children do believe in punishment. The strong belief in expiatory punishment yielded to belief in punishment by reciprocity, but a belief in punishment remained. What we see here, then, is that when equality or distributive justice conflicts with retribution, equality outweighs retribution.

There are three stages in development in children's reasoning about situations where retributive punishment and distributive justice are in conflict. Most of the younger children, ages six to nine, believe that punishment supersedes notions of distributive justice. If each child in a group has been given a balloon, and one child while playing breaks his, he should not be given another. He should suffer the punishment of having broken his balloon. The very young child would probably even add another punishment to this! Children ages nine to twelve focus on equality. The child who broke a balloon should be given another, so that each of the children will still have one. The mother should give the same size piece of cake to both girls. Justice for this age child is a strict, calculating equality. The older children, ages twelve to fourteen, make their decisions on consideration of equity, which Piaget describes as "equality allowing for the circumstances of each."[12] These children weigh considerations of age, relationships of affection, and past experiences. They temper strict equality with notions of what is the nice thing to do.

What happens then as these developing notions of justice come into conflict with adult authority? Does adult authority diminish in importance and influence as justice gains ascendancy? Piaget states that "justice has no meaning except as something that is above authority."[13] By probing children's reasoning in situations where fairness conflicted with obedience to authority, Piaget found three broad stages of development to the autonomy required for the development of justice. It is useful to reprint the four stories used for probing children's thoughts, because with slight vocabulary modifications they represent typical family and school situations.[14]

1. Once there was a camp for Boy Scouts (or Girl Scouts). Each one had to do his bit to help with the work and leave things tidy. One had to do the shopping, another brought in wood or swept the floor. One day there was no bread and the one who did the shopping had already gone. So the Scoutmaster asked one of the Scouts who had already done his job to go and fetch the bread. What did he do?
2. One Thursday afternoon, a mother asked her little girl and boy to help her around the house because she was tired. The girl was to dry the plates and the boy was to fetch some wood. But the little boy (or girl) went out and played in the street, so the mother asked the other one to do all the work. What did he (she) say?
3. Once there was a family with three brothers. The two

younger brothers were twins. They all used to polish their shoes every morning. One day the oldest brother was ill, so the mother asked one of the others to polish the brother's shoes as well as his own. What do you think of that?

4. A father had two boys. One of them always grumbled when he was sent on messages. The other one didn't like being sent either, but he always went without saying a word. So the father used to send the boy who didn't grumble more often than the other one. What do you think of that?

The younger children insist on obedience. "What is just is not differentiated from what is in conformity to authority."[15] Some of the younger children can distinguish between what is just and what is commanded, but the command nevertheless should be obeyed, even if it is unfair, because an authority has given it. At the lowest stage, then, "justice is what is law." "Just is what is commanded by the adult."[16] At the next stage equality overrules obedience. If commands are unfair, the children who are commanded should not carry them out. They might have to because adults could force them, but if the command is unfair the children should not respond to it. The typical response, familiar to all who have dealt with children, and emanating from this stage of reasoning, is "No, I won't clean it up; I didn't make the mess" or "Why do I have to close the door? I wasn't the last one in." These children count "an eye for an eye, and a tooth for a tooth." An important fact for adults to remember, even though one may long for the earlier docile days, is that this is a stage of development, and it is development toward moral autonomy. The child at this age is struggling with the confrontation of his developing notions of justice and his unilateral respect for adult authority. Though easier times are recalled, one should take heart because better days are coming. The third stage is a stage of equity "which consists in never defining equality without taking account of the way in which each individual is situated."[17] At this stage the child recognizes unjust commands and labels them as unfair, but he doesn't see that as the only factor to be considered in determining whether he will comply with a command; he also considers various relationships, such as age, friendliness and affection. Contrast this with the child at the second stage who equates unfairness with non-compliance. The child governed by considerations of equity may obey the command, but obedience is freely chosen. His reasons for obeying are not "you should do what adults tell you," but "it would be a nice thing to do" or "to please my mother." The command is placed in a context of various relationships and past experiences with the one commanding. It would seem that at this stage children who are responding "to be nice" would be helped by receiving due recognition for that. Adult respect for the child's right not to respond to a clearly unfair demand should also be conveyed. Children, like adults, do not always feel like being nice. Although a manifestation of adult superior force may yield compliance, such coercion in an unfair demand will not facilitate development.

The stages of justice and authority are diagrammed in Table IV.

TABLE IV.   Stages of Justice and Authority

Ages	5	6	7	8	9	10	11	12	13	14
Equity—considers other factors								▇	▇	▇
Equality outweighs obedience, even friendliness					▇	▇	▇	▇		
Just is what is commanded	▇	▇	▇	▇						

Children's development in the authority-justice relationships is painful for adults and probably for the children. I think this is a crucial phase of moral development and that it affects autonomy in all other areas. This was revealed clearly in interviews with four seventh and eighth graders. I told the children the following story from Kohlberg:[18]

Joe is a fourteen year old boy who wanted to go to camp very much. His father promised him he could go if he saved up the money for it himself. So Joe worked hard at his paper route and saved up the $40 it cost to go to camp and a little more besides. But, just before camp was going to start, his father changed his mind. Some of his friends decided to go on a special fishing trip, and Joe's father was short of the money it would cost. So he told Joe to give him the money he had saved from the paper route. Joe didn't want to give up going to camp, so he thought of refusing to give his father the money. Should Joe refuse to give his father the money or should he give it to him? Why?

I was looking for responses from the children that would indicate where these children were in their development in authority-justice relationships. Lynn, a twelve year old, recognized the father's demand as unfair, but felt that Joe ought to give the father the money to be nice. Joe did not have to give the father the money, but it would be nice. Lynn's responses indicated a third stage reasoning, equity. Peter, a thirteen year old, responded strongly from a stage two equality mentality: Joe should "refuse to give the money," "the kid earned it; the father has no right to demand it." Both these responses indicate normal development in sorting out demands of justice and authority, but Lynn has developed farther than Peter.

However, Jimmy, a fourteen year old, thinks "Joe should give the money to his father"; "the father has a right to ask for it"; "Joe should respect his father." A child of fourteen responding from what appears to be a low stage in authority-justice relationships is *retarded* in his moral development, and this is bound to cause problems for him in school and home. Jimmy still operates under a morality of constraint where things should be done because an adult commands them. But we know from our earlier examination of children's notions of rules that there is a gap between this heteronomous respect for rules and the practice of them. An examination of Jimmy's school record on character evaluation indicates that his compliance to school directives and his personal responsibility are problem areas. Possibly Jimmy lives in a very authoritarian family structure where he often hears the command "you do it or else," because his response to a command of parental authority is one of unquestioning obedience. A child needs latitude and support to develop his critical powers and to apply these to his parents' commands and actions. This is not easy for parents, but it is an essential part of the pain of raising children to moral autonomy. Jimmy will slink along, outwardly submissive when his actions are obvious, but never freely choosing obedience. In fact Jimmy would be closer to the first son in the Gospel story of the father who told one son to "do this" and the son said "Yes, father" and went off never doing it, as contrasted with the second son who complained and said "No," but did it anyway.

Piaget found that ascendancy in the influence of notions of equality over authority affected other areas of justice which he also explored. Almost all the children interviewed felt it was unfair to keep children waiting in a store until all the adults were waited on. "Everyone should be taken in turn" and "Children might be in a hurry too" were typical responses. Only the youngest children had any hesitancy about this.

Children's notions of why one should not cheat develop from indications of adult constraint in responses like "It's wrong," "You'll be punished," and "You shouldn't," to indications of judgments based on equality in responses like "You ought to find out for yourself" and "It isn't fair; it's his work." As equality grows stronger, reasons based on adult prohibitions decrease. Rules are critically examined and the child develops his own reasons for living by them.

Similarly, when asked whether children should tell on each other if an adult commands it, the younger children respond in favor of authority. They say: "It's O.K. to tell" and "The father should be told." From about age eight on, however, the rule of authority has diminished in this regard and the eight year old responds: "He should tell nothing. It would be rotten to tell on your brother." This perspective does not come without a struggle. There is a period where the child wavers between equality and authority and cannot easily resolve the dilemma.

It is not difficult to understand why moral education programs formulated without knowledge of children's developmental stages have not been successful. Piaget's studies have indicated that the most serious obstacle to moral development in early childhood is the child's relationship of respect for and dependence on adults, because it results in a morality of submission to their rules. As we have seen, the only intention the young child has is to conform to adult rules, but these are peripheral to his conscience; they are forces directing him, rather than internalized motivating principles.

We will discuss in a later chapter the educational implications of these findings. At this point, let us review once again the mindset of the young child.

Moral realism is a natural quality of child thought. He sees a world order which includes physical laws, biological laws and all the rules and regulations of his own life, and he does not make any distinctions between the laws of the universe and those rules that regulate his life, nor between the moral rules of stealing and lying and the disciplinary regulations in his life, such as washing his hands before dinner and wiping his feet before coming into the house. All laws for him exist by themselves, independent of the mind, independent of circumstances and of intentions. He thinks there must be a reason for them in the total world order.

We saw in his judgments about responsibility and punishment that the problem of determining guilt is a simple one for him. The question is only to know whether a law has been violated. In the physical order if he trips and falls, he violates a physical law, so to speak, and it has immediate consequences; no intention is considered. Similarly, violating the law of lying or stealing or spoiling must have consequences and intention is not a consideration. In fact, as we saw in his views on immanent justice, if the fault goes unnoticed, "things" will punish the violator.

This natural tendency of the young child toward moral realism is also a product of adult constraint. The source of moral obligation and sense of duty stems from the child's respect for adults. Every command is an obligatory rule, because he cannot differentiate and order what adults ask of him. Therefore, the unilateral respect of the child for the adult, combined with a natural tendency toward moral realism, forms a morality of heteronomy.

In the stages of definitions of a lie we could see clearly the process of reason working over a heteronomous rule, taking it from "anything that is not true" to "something intentionally false," eventually generalizing it and making it universally applicable. This is morality of autonomy, and the most significant factor in its development is cooperation because it forces the child to be occupied with the point of view of other people. The autonomy of Piaget's eleven and twelve year olds refers to a freedom from heteronomy. Quoting from Bovet, Piaget explains how personal autonomy comes to be conquered: "Reason works over moral rules, as she works over everything, generalizing them, making them coherent with each other, and above all extending them progressively to all individuals until universality is reached."[19] Obviously this is a lifelong process, merely begun by the twelve year old.

Summary

In summary then, Piaget, in his analysis of game rules, has shown that children go through a stage of professing reverence for game rules while their play demonstrates mere imitation of some aspects of the game and no understanding of the game in terms of all of its rules. At this stage the child is conscious that rules exist, but all rules are external to his mind, like a maze of constraints governing his every movement. As the child develops socially and intellectually there is a corresponding development in both his knowledge of the rules and his understanding of games in terms of rules.

In the sections on clumsiness and stealing and on lying, a similar developmental process was traced. Children's consciousness of rules about breakage, theft and language precedes their understanding of the rules and their ability to apply them in various circumstances. The additional factor complicating development in the moral life is the child's respect for adults who both articulate and enforce the moral rules for the young child. In the stages where the child is merely conscious of these rules, without understanding them, his judgments of right and wrong are based on the letter of the rule. As the child develops intellectually and socially, moral rules, referring to stealing, cheating and lying, are understood in the context of community life and then become internalized principles.

The sections on children's notions of justice reveal clearly the influence of adults on children's definitions of right and wrong, and the confrontation with adult authority that is essential for development to autonomy. The young child equates fairness with whatever an adult asks or commands. As he develops intellectually and socially, his judgments on fairness are made strictly in terms of equality, without consideration of other relationships, such as affection or age or physical condition. This is a period of radical separation from adult authority. The third stage in the development of justice, the stage of equity, is characterized by the desire to weigh all of the relationships and circumstances before making decisions in questions of justice. At this point the child has freed himself from the influence of external forces and he is autonomous in his moral judgment.

II
Kohlberg's Theory
of Moral Development

Besides Piaget, who is the recognized pioneer in the psychology of moral development, perhaps the most important psychologist in the field is Lawrence Kohlberg, whose research has complemented as well as expanded on that of Piaget. Kohlberg is an American who is currently professor of education and social psychology at Harvard University where he carries on and directs an extensive amount of research in moral development. He was educated at the University of Chicago, to which he returned as a teacher and researcher in child psychology after spending a few years at Yale and the Institute for Advanced Studies in the Behavioral Sciences, Palo Alto, California. He left Chicago in 1967 for Harvard, where along with his teaching and research he directs an institute which is designed to acquaint fellow professionals with his theories and research tools.

In the initial phase of his research, Kohlberg selected a group of fifty American males ranging in age from ten to twenty eight, and interviewed them every three years for a period of eighteen years. Initially, he identified six generally distinguishable orientations or perspectives which became the basis for his six stages of moral development. Over eighteen years, Kohlberg found that each of his subjects went through the same sequence of stages, although the rate of development differed and all subjects had not reached the highest stages of moral development. In addition to interviewing the group of fifty, Kohlberg and others using his system and techniques have interviewed subjects from other cultures as well as more subjects from America. Such interviewing continues to support the soundness of Kohlberg's theories.

The interview involves the presentation of a moral situation or a moral dilemma, and the asking of questions designed to uncover the reasons for the subjects' recommending specific courses of action in such situations. This concentration on the subjects' reasons for recommending a specific course of action is the hallmark of the kind of research that Kohlberg carries on, and it is important to distinguish it from research which concentrates on moral behavior.

Kohlberg, like Piaget, does not concentrate on moral behavior. That is, he does not concern himself with what an individual is *doing*. Studying behavior does not tell much about moral maturity. After all a mature adult and a young child may both resist stealing an apple. In such a situation their behavior is the same. But if there is a difference in their moral maturity, their behavior doesn't indicate it; the reasons for not stealing it do. What is more, Kohlberg does not concern himself with people's *statements* about whether an action is right or wrong. The reason is similar to the previous one. A mature adult as well as a young child may *say* that stealing an apple is wrong. Here again there seems to be no difference between the adult and the child. What do show differences in moral maturity are the *reasons given why* stealing an apple is wrong. These reasons are the indicators of the levels or stages of moral maturity. It is more informative to look at the reasons a person thinks an action is wrong than it is to look at the person's action (behavior) or even to listen to what the person says is wrong (statement).

Kohlberg's research showed that when one looks at the reasons a person gives for his moral judgments or moral actions, significant differences in people's moral outlook become apparent. Whereas one person might indicate that cheating is wrong because one can get caught doing it, another person might indicate that cheating undermines the trust necessary to preserve society. Here a significant difference in the maturity of the reasoning process and in the reasons given is obvious.

In order to develop a systematic tool for uncovering reasons, Kohlberg developed a set of stories (cf. Appendix) which involve a person or persons in a moral dilemma. He then set up questions about the dilemmas which were designed to probe for the subject's reasons for recommending specific courses of action in such situations. For purposes of illustration, let us relate one of Kohlberg's stories, known to students of Kohlberg as the Heinz dilemma. (Cf. Appendix II for all of Kohlberg's Moral Judgment Situations.)

Story II. In Europe, a woman was near death from a special kind of cancer. There was one drug that the doctors thought might save her. It was a form of radium that a druggist in the same town had recently discovered. The drug was expensive to make, but the druggist was charging ten times the amount the drug had cost him to make. He paid $200 for the radium and charged $2,000 for a small dose of the drug. The sick woman's husband, Heinz, went to everyone he knew to borrow the money, but he could only get together about $1,000, which is half of what it cost. He told the druggist that his wife was dying and asked him to sell it cheaper or let him pay later. The druggist said, "No, I discovered the drug and I'm going to make money from it." So Heinz got desperate, and broke into the man's store to steal the drug for his wife.

Some of the questions asked about the story are the following: Should Heinz steal the drug? Why? Which is worse, letting someone die or stealing? Why? What does the value of life mean to you? Is there a good reason for a husband to steal if he doesn't love his wife? Would it be as right to steal for a stranger as to steal for his wife? If Heinz is caught, should he be sent to prison? If Heinz is caught and brought to trial, should the judge sentence him? Why? What is the responsibility of the judge to society in this case?

Besides developing the stories and the probe questions, Kohlberg has devised scoring systems which allow researchers to organize varying answers to such questions about the Heinz dilemma and other dilemmas. The scoring system indicates which stage or level of moral development the subject has reached. It is important to emphasize at this point that no one answer to one dilemma or even a host of answers to one dilemma need yield enough data for determining which stage a subject has reached. A researcher should cover the whole range of dilemmas and seek answers to the variety of probe questions. Somewhere along the way a pattern of responses will emerge and an evaluation as to the stage of a subject can be made. For example, in our own interviewing of two eighth graders we gave them the Heinz dilemma. A boy who seemed to be quite liberal in his justification of Heinz' stealing of the drug and the judge's being lenient by giving him no sentence at all showed, upon probing, that this liberality was justified mostly in terms of pleasure and pain. A girl classmate, who was noticeably less liberal in justifying Heinz' behavior, showed, upon probing, much more sensitivity to ideals and a respect for the law, and almost no concern with pleasure and pain, which indicated a level of reasoning different and, as we shall see shortly, higher than the boy's reasoning. The point of the example is simply to underline the fact that when one probes a dilemma with different questions from different perspectives one begins to see clearly different patterns of response. These different patterns indicate different orientations which in turn are the basis for postulating various stages of moral reasoning.

Kohlberg's Moral Judgment Stages

Kohlberg identified six stages, two stages occurring at three distinct levels—the pre-conventional, the conventional and the post-conventional.

Pre-Conventional Level

At this level the child is responsive to cultural rules and labels of good and bad, right or wrong, but interprets these labels in terms of either the physical or the hedonistic consequences of action (punishment, reward, exchange of favors) or in terms of the physical power of those who enunciate the rules and labels. The level is divided into two stages:

State 1: The Punishment and Obedience Orientation. The physical consequences of action determine its goodness or badness regardless of the human meaning or value of these consequences. Avoidance of punishment and unquestioning deference to power are valued in their own right, not in terms of respect for an underlying moral order supported by punishment and authority (the latter being Stage 4).

Stage 2: The Instrumental Relativist Orientation. Right action consists of that which instrumentally satisfies one's own needs and occasionally the needs of others. Human relations are viewed in terms like those of the marketplace. Elements of fairness, reciprocity, and equal sharing are present, but they are always interpreted in a physical or pragmatic way. Reciprocity is a matter of "you scratch my back and I'll scratch yours," not of loyalty, gratitude, or justice.

Conventional Level

At this level, maintaining the expectations of the individual's family, group, or nation is perceived as valuable in its own right, regardless of immediate and obvious consequences. The attitude is not only one of conformity to personal expectations and social order, but of loyalty to it, of actively maintaining, supporting, and justifying the order and of identifying with the persons or group involved in it. At this level, there are two stages:

Stage 3: The Interpersonal Concordance of "Good Boy—Nice Girl" Orientation. Good behavior is that which pleases or helps others and is approved by them. There is much conformity to stereotypical images of what is majority or "natural" behavior. Behavior is frequently judged by intention: "He means well" becomes important for the first time. One earns approval by being "nice."

Stage 4: The Law and Order Orientation. There is orientation toward authority, fixed rules, and the maintenance of the social order. Right behavior consists of doing one's duty, showing respect for authority and maintaining the given social order for its own sake.

Post-Conventional, Autonomous, or Principled Level

At this level, there is a clear effort to define moral values and principles which have validity and application apart from the authority of the groups or persons holding these principles and apart from the individual's own identification with these groups. This level has two stages:

Stage 5: The Social-Contract Legalistic Orientation. Generally with utilitarian overtones. Right action tends to be defined in terms of general individual rights and in terms of standards which have been critically examined and agreed upon by the whole society. There is a clear awareness of the relativism of personal values and opinions and a corresponding emphasis upon procedural rules for reaching consensus. Aside from what is constitutionally and democratically agreed upon, the right is a matter of personal values and opinion. The result is an emphasis upon the legal point of view, but with an emphasis upon the possibility of changing law in terms of rational considerations of social utility (rather than rigidly maintaining it in terms of Stage 4 law and order). Outside the legal realm, free agreement and contract is the binding element of obligation. This is the "official" morality of the American government and Constitution.

Stage 6: The Universal Ethical Principle Orientation. Right is defined by the decision of conscience in accord with self-chosen ethical principles appealing to logical comprehensiveness, universality, and consistency. These principles are abstract and ethical (the golden rule, the categorical imperative) and are not concrete moral rules like the ten commandments. At heart, these are universal principles of justice, of the reciprocity and equality of the human rights, and of respect for the dignity of human beings as individual persons.[1]

Our main task in the rest of this chapter will be to elaborate on these definitions of each stage, indicating the relationships between them primarily by emphasizing the changes that take place in the development from one stage to another. However, before beginning such an elaboration it is necessary to mention four qualities of stage development which have been reinforced by Kohlberg's studies.

1. *Stage development is invariant.* One must progress through the stages in order, and one cannot get to a higher stage without

passing through the stage immediately preceding it. Thus, one cannot get to stage four without passing through stages one, two and three respectively. This will become more apparent as we describe the transitions from one stage to another, but for now try to imagine the sort of mental adjustment which would be required for someone who looks at the good in terms of pleasure for himself, to suddenly adopt an orientation where he looks at the good in terms of an abstract system of rights and obligations. A belief that such a leap into moral maturity is possible is in sharp contrast to the facts of developmental research. Moral development is growth and, like all growth, takes place according to a pre-determined sequence. To expect someone to grow into high moral maturity overnight would be like expecting someone to walk before he crawls.

2. *In stage development, subjects cannot comprehend moral reasoning at a stage more than one stage beyond their own.* Thus a person at stage two, who discriminates good and bad on the basis of his own pleasure, cannot comprehend reasoning at stage four which appeals to fixed duties the performance of which need not offer any promise of reward or pleasure. Since stage four reasoning requires an orientation quite different from stage two reasoning, a series of cognitive readjustments must be made in order for stage four reasoning to be comprehended. If Johnny is oriented to see good almost exclusively as that which brings him satisfaction, how will he understand a concept of the good in which the good might bring him no pleasure at all, indeed might even cause him pain? The moral maxim "It is better to give than to receive" reflects a high state of moral maturity and development. But it is incomprehensible to someone at a low level of moral development. The child who honestly asks you why it is better to give than to receive does so because he does not and cannot understand such thinking. The reason is simply that he cannot comprehend thinking more than one stage above his own. To his mind "better" means "better for him," and how can it be better for him to give than to receive?

3. *In stage development subjects are cognitively attracted to reasoning one level above their own predominant level.* A stage one person will be attracted by stage two reasoning, a stage two person by stage three reasoning, and so on. Kohlberg asserts that

reasoning at higher stages is cognitively more adequate than reasoning at lower stages, since it resolves problems and dilemmas in a more satisfactory way. Since reasoning at one stage higher is intelligible and since it makes more sense and resolves more difficulties, it is more attractive. If one is operating from an orientation where he thinks that it would be good for him to get the whole piece of pie, even while his bigger and stronger brother insists on getting the whole piece of pie, some thought about sharing, which is a higher stage of reasoning, will be a more attractive solution of the dilemma than the solution which would occur if both insisted on the pie and the stronger brother got it.

4. *In stage development, movement through the stages is effected when cognitive disequilibrium is created*, that is, when a person's cognitive outlook is not adequate to cope with a given moral dilemma. The belief of developmental theory, bolstered by the evidence, is that a person will look for more and more adequate ways of resolving dilemmas. If in a given situation one's cognitive framework cannot resolve a problem, the cognitive organism adjusts to a framework which does. Yet if a person's orientation is not disturbed (there is no cognitive disequilibrium) there is no reason to expect any development. Thus, in the apple pie example, if the bigger and stronger brother wants the pie he can have it and there is no dilemma. Only if he puts himself in the younger brother's place will he be forced to examine his self-interested point of view. For the smaller brother, however, the realization that the bigger brother will get the pie unless there is some other procedure of distribution will effect a questioning of the self-interested viewpoint. A different solution of the problem will be sought. When such a disequilibrium is provoked, it causes thinking about the inadequacies of one's reasons and a search for better and more adequate reasons.

These qualities of stage development are, as we said, important to keep in mind. They have not only been verified time and again by research but they also make sense if one looks at the development of one's cognitive capacity as a kind of orderly growth. Moral development, like all other natural growth, follows a definite pattern.

Our exposition of Kohlberg's stages will attempt to keep these qualities in mind, particularly the last two, for we will attempt to describe how a person at any specific stage reaches disequilibrium how that person finds the next higher stage cognitively more adequate in resolving a dilemma, and why that next higher stage will be more attractive.

Besides these qualities of stage development, Kohlberg also points out another important general characteristic about the process of moral development which will govern our presentation. According to Kohlberg, up through stage four each stage represents a wider and more adequate perception of the social system and an ability to think more abstractly.[2] In our account we will describe each stage, indicate its inadequacies, and show how the next higher stage compensates for these inadequacies by being a more adequate view of the social system. We will also show how such a view requires less concrete and more abstract thinking.

Turning our attention to the six stages listed in the table, we see that Kohlberg arranges them in pairs, locating each pair in one of three levels which he names respectively the "pre-conventional," "conventional" and "post-conventional" levels. The orientations characteristic of these levels reflect specific differences in the wideness of the view of the social system and differences in one's ability to think beyond one's immediate concrete situation.

Society and groups, whether we take note of it or not, are not concrete things like individual people, discernible to the senses. To appreciate the existence of a group requires an ability to think in an abstract way and, as we saw in Piaget, the ability to shed egocentrism and to see oneself as a member of a group. Each movement from level to level results from a different perspective of groups and one's relationship to groups. Thus while reasoning at the first two stages, the pre-conventional level, involves quite concrete reasoning about individual persons and events, with little or no perception of a society, its groups or institutions, reasoning at the third and fourth stages, the conventional level, involves gradually more abstract thinking in which a perception of society, its groups and its institutions develops.

At this point, we conclude our preliminary remarks and turn to an examination of the specific levels and stages which Kohlberg discovered.

Kohlberg characterizes the pre-conventional level, which includes stages one and two, as a level wherein "the child is responsive to cultural rules and labels of good and bad, right and wrong, but interprets these labels in terms of either the physical or the hedonistic consequences of action (punishment, reward, exchange of favors) or in terms of the physical power of those who enunciate the rules and labels."[3] By and large the pre-conventional level includes pre-adolescent children (ages 10-13), although it may include some adults who have been fixated in their development. Since adults fixated at this level are an exception, we will talk mainly, as does Kohlberg, about children.

At the pre-conventional level, when a child hears that something is good or bad, he has a very different picture of the thing than you or I (unless, that is, we are fixated at level one). When Johnny says that "cheating is bad," what he is saying is either that "cheating will lead to punishment" or that "cheating will not bring me any rewards" or perhaps "the teacher says not to cheat, and she is in league with my parents and they are all bigger than me, and if I cheat, I will get jerked back like before."

The child at this level has a very narrow view of society gained from his own concrete experiences. Some actions he performs bring pain, like touching a burning match. Others bring pleasure, like eating ice cream. Some actions which involve others also bring pain, in the form of punishment, such as when he breaks a lamp; others bring pleasure, such as when he gets an "A" in school. He simply judges actions in terms of expected consequences. Some of the consequences are natural, but others come from other people (society). He is small, weak, and dependent on others in society for receiving a good deal of pleasure and/or pain. Hence, he is psychologically disposed to view himself as an inferior in an authority relationship and to defer to those in authority (they being identified concretely for him as those who have the power to employ sanctions to control his actions), because they are the instruments of pleasure and pain in his life.

Children live under rules they have no say in developing. The rules, so far as the child knows, were always there. He sees no value in the rules themselves; they are simply indicators of what behavior will bring pleasure and what behavior will bring pain.

This gives rise to an egoism (a concern for oneself) that reflects a lack of a feeling of identity with society or a group.

To view things other than egoistically requires a level of abstraction which attributes a unity to a societal group that goes beyond what the child has experienced. The child's experience has been simply that of himself as an individual reacting to an environment that is other than he is, including things, and to people. To move out of egoism to a state of identifying with a society and its norms, one must develop the ability to role play, that is, the ability to put oneself in another's place. Until one intellectually puts oneself in another's place, one cannot really comprehend what a society is or feel what it means to be a part of society. And by and large, what it means to be a part of society is to begin to see that the rules have a purpose and are not just arbitrary constraints imposed on a child.

At the pre-conventional level, then, one feels like an outsider against society (society not construed as a unit, but more as distinct individuals who subject him to rules). The child's experience is that older people are tougher, bigger, and different. To view these older people as being like him demands an abstraction. What the child has experienced is that older people seem to know things he does not. They know what to do, are always telling him, and are always seeming to say that what looks like fun is bad. The reasoning pattern, then, which would filter a child's perceptions would be such that when he hears an adult say that something is wrong, he would hear an implied threat that it will bring unpleasant consequences.

Let us reinforce an earlier point here. We have been talking solely about children's views. It would, however, be a mistake to think that only children reason morally at stage one or two. Some adults do. Kohlberg has done some studies with prisoners and found some at a level one of reasoning. Although cognitive ability and consequently some chronological age growth is a necessary condition for stage development, it is not a sufficient condition, and consequently some adults might still think at the pre-conventional level.

Thus far, we have been talking in general about the characteristics of reasoning at the pre-conventional level. Yet, there are two stages in this level. Let us turn our attention specifically to stage one, the punishment and obedience orientation. According to Kohlberg, in stage one the "physical consequences of an action determine its goodness or badness regardless of the human meaning or value of these consequences." No matter what we value in the action, the child at stage one doesn't see that value; he just sees us approving or disapproving of it, and that is enough to indicate to him that it ought to be pursued or avoided, because if it is not, the adult will not like it. Thus, as Kohlberg continues, "avoidance of punishment and unquestioning deference to power are valued in their own right, not in terms of respect for an underlying moral order supported by punishment and authority." There it is. At this stage the child is afraid of punishment. Fear generates his values.

If you think the orientation and world view at this stage is undesirable, you are correct. It is obvious that one would want to move a child out of this stage as swiftly as possible. However, there is a practical deterrent. Children who respond to fear of punishment present us with a conveniently docile subject from whom we can easily extract "proper behavior."

I remember a story my grandfather used to tell about three boys who constantly harassed an old man as he walked to the village from his home. On the way was a deep, dense wood. The boys would taunt, jeer, and throw stones, and the old man was helpless, suffering greatly from the children's behavior. One day, while the boys were taunting him in a cruel way, he hurried into the woods and disappeared into a thicket. Shortly after, there was a loud crack of thunder in the direction the old man had gone and a bear came charging out of the spot. My grandfather assured us that the old man had miraculously turned into the bear. The end of the story is rather grizzly. The bear ate the boys. The moral of the story was very clear: "Respect your elders, or else. . . ."

Two points about the story. It was very effective for getting children to respect their elders, particularly when one was at stage one. But a counterpoint concerns the value of such stories. Although they may help children achieve cultural conformity, they don't help to advance the level of one's moral reasoning. They don't ask why the rule "Respect your elders" is a good rule; they simply exact obedience. As we mentioned, Kohlberg found a real willingness to accept a stage of reasoning one step higher than the predominant stage of one's thinking because the higher stage was cognitively more adequate. So, if a person is at stage one, he can be attracted by stage two thinking.

We will look at a stage two version of the story shortly, but we cannot help calling attention to the fact that so many fables and children's stories teach that the villain is destroyed. One must wonder about the pedagogic value of such stories. Think of all the stories where the witch gets melted (Wizard of Oz) or cooked (Hansel and Gretel), or where the villain gets shot (the wolf in Little Red Riding Hood or The Three Little Pigs). Recall also the religious practices which evoke obedience by threatening eternal damnation or everlasting fire. There is a particularly graphic scene in the film "Inherit the Wind," the film about the Scopes monkey trial, where the preacher, scandalized that his daughter would associate with the teacher who was advocating the evolutionary theory, cursed her to eternal damnation for her sins. It is a particularly frightening scene, but indicative of an appeal to a level one reasoning. These stories and practices are not calculated to raise one's level of reasoning; rather, they reinforce stage one by reiterating the rule and pointing out the painful consequences of breaking it.

A better story, more uplifting than the bear story, would be one where another boy challenged the nasty boys who were taunting the old man and stood up to them. A fight ensued, but the boy, even though he got scraped and battered, managed to drive the sadistic boys off. At that point, the old man turned out to be a very, very rich man who bought the "good" little boy candy and goodies, and even took him and his poor mother to live in his mansion. Here the motive for goodness changes from fear of punishment to hope of reward. Does it not seem reasonable that a child who does things out of fear would respond much more readily to promises of reward? Does it not also seem reasonable that if I help someone they are likely to help me back? Of course it does, and this is precisely what happens. Identifying the good with what promises reward, and the realization that if I scratch your back you'll scratch mine, is characteristic of the second stage of moral reasoning.

Kohlberg calls stage two the instrumental relativist orientation. The subject in stage two characterizes right action as "that which instrumentally satisfies one's own needs and occasionally the needs of others." "Human relations are viewed in terms like those of the marketplace; elements of fairness, reciprocity and equal sharing are present, but they are always interpreted in a physical or pragmatic way. Reciprocity is a matter of 'you scratch my back and I'll scratch yours,' not of loyalty, gratitude or justice.' "[4]

A little reflection indicates two major advances over stage one thinking, a more positive conception of what is good and a more adequate view of society, both, however, tempered by egoism. The stage two person can be viewed as a hedonist, a pleasure seeker.

Whereas the good in stage one thinking was characterized negatively as the avoidance of pain, in stage two it is characterized more positively as the pleasant consequences that accrue to an action. This is a much more optimistic, less awful view of the universe. "Do this because the reward will be great" is the moral imperative at this stage. Goodness takes on a positive face. Yet, at this stage, judgment is still quite concrete, dealing with this particular action and the expected consequences, as well as still quite egoistic, that is, the consequences have to be pleasant for the subject.

Along with this more optimistic view which identifies the good as something which fills one's needs rather than the avoidance of that which frustrates them, there is a more adequate view of one's relation to other human beings than is found in stage one. Although as in stage one the chief determination of what is good is still self-interest, the view of society is no longer solely that of a group of authorities having control over the individual, but as a group comprised of individuals like oneself. If this is so, then the chances are that if I help someone, they are likely to help me. This does not mean that authority plays no role in the stage two person's considerations, since it is a fact that there are authorities and these authorities can be viewed as instruments for reward or punishment. Nevertheless, at stage two, the person begins to recognize that people are all in the same boat and that if we work together we can help each other. It begins to look pragmatic to join together cooperatively with others, since that will be "instrumental" in one's gaining pleasure for oneself.

This notion of "reciprocity," of "you scratch my back and I'll scratch yours," reflects a wider view of society and its rules than we find in stage one, and it is a rudimentary move toward socialization. Let us trace the kind of process that takes place in leading to it.

This stage occurs most times in pre-adolescence, and it is at this age that one concretely begins to experience that those in authority make mistakes too. They may be bigger and stronger, but they are not supermen or superwomen. Their kisses really do not make hurts feel better, and my father may not be better than your father. Parents fall off the pedestals they were on, and it becomes thinkable that somebody else's parents would be preferable to ours. Along with this concrete realization that authorities are not all wise and all powerful, a new perspective of society as a whole comes with the developing ability to put oneself in the place of another. When one puts oneself in another's place, one gains, if not a feeling of superiority over another, at least a view of the other as being fundamentally equal to oneself. A child, at this stage, sees himself for the first time as an individual equal to others. If authorities make mistakes, then they are like him. If they are like him, then so is everybody else. If we are all alike, why should one person have more rights than another? This is the basic perspective of fairness which is the stage two person's orientation. Doesn't it explain the adamant insistence of so many youngsters on fairness? It is only too easy to come up with examples of young people who will challenge their elders with cries of indignation, such as: "Joey had an ice cream cone, so I deserve one too." The attitude reflects not only a lessening of the fear of authority, but also, and more importantly, an elementary sense of equal sharing, fairness and reciprocity. Still such an attitude is hardly informed by any sense of willingness to share which would be characteristic of a higher level and more communal spirit. The level of thinking is still fairly concrete. A group is a collection of individuals, each one of whom is viewed as reasoning as the stage two person does—concretely in terms of their needs. What a stage two perception makes one realize is that concrete fulfillment of needs and desires is to be preferred to punishment. It stands to reason that others think the same way. It does not occur to a stage two person that someone would give up his pleasures for the sake of a group. Basically, the stage two person wants "his" first, but because he now sees others as having wants and needs like his own, he can appreciate that others might like to get "theirs," and that perhaps two or more can work together so that all are satisfied.

To focus a little more sharply on stage two and its differences from stage one, let us recall Kohlberg's story about Joe which we mentioned in our treatment of Piaget. Recall that Joe is a fourteen year old boy who wanted to go to camp very much and his father told Joe to give him his money so that he (the father) could go on a fishing trip.

One finds a striking contrast between stage one and stage two responses. The stage one response will concur with giving the father the money, obviously because the father is an all-powerful figure. The stage two response, however, will probably be opposed to giving the money to the father because the demand is "unjust." What injustice in this context means is this: Since there is no advantage for Joe in giving the money to his father, there is nothing good about giving it away. Also, since the father is an individual like Joe, he has no claim to the money simply because he is a father. However, in one of our interviews, a boy at stage two advised giving the money to his father. His reason is illuminating. He reasoned that the father might want the money to give Joe a surprise. This illustrates an obedience not determined by a fear of punishment but by a hope of reward, a belief that, perhaps, if he helps his father, his father will reward him.

It is important to note that if a stage two person is allowed to respond honestly to dilemmas, he will often give answers we do not expect. They will be egoistic and devoid of considerations of self-sacrifice. The stage two individual may shock people inclined to accept only answers based on altruism. Our eighth grade boy, whom we mentioned earlier, could only measure values in terms of personal pleasure and thus could only justify Heinz' stealing the drug for his wife on the grounds that she was his wife and "instrumental" to his happiness. He could not justify stealing the drug for someone Heinz did not know on broader humanitarian (or should we say Good Samaritan) grounds. To steal for a stranger or even a neighbor held no promise of pleasure; hence it was not right to do it.

In terms of pragmatically dealing with stage two people, the most effective means, of course, is to get them to think that something is going to benefit them. If fear and punishment worked before, if one could appeal to the wrongness of an action by predicting hell at stage one, the promise of eternal bliss will be much more effective at stage two. Either way, however, on the pre-conventional level, the fundamental characteristic is an egoism or self-interest which arises from a cognitive disposition to judge things completely according to their consequences.

It has often occurred to me that a child at stage two must find some of our more ideal maxims quite confusing. I remember having a good deal of difficulty as a child comprehending the maxim we mentioned above, "It is better to give than to receive." That just seemed painfully stupid to me at the time. I was being sold a bill of goods, although since authority was saying so, I wouldn't have dared to challenge it. But isn't it the case that for someone at a stage two perspective, if such a maxim is not stupid, it is at least incomprehensible? From a stage two perspective, when one says an action is better it means that that action is going to yield more pleasure for the agent. If, then, I am the agent and am told it is better to give than receive, I am being told (or at least I hear): "Give so you can get more," or "The more you give the more you get." But, of course, this prediction rarely comes true. The stage two person then must feel deceived by such a maxim, for at that stage it is obvious that it is better to receive than to give.

However, there may come a point when stage two reasoning is inadequate. (Once more it is good to remember that there are adults who still think at stage two.) Suppose that needs conflict, as for example Heinz' and the druggist's, or Joe's and his father's. Is there any way to adjudicate the conflict?

We already saw our eighth grade boy trying to resolve the father's "unjust" demand for the money by not facing the facts, by wishing or hoping the father really wanted it to buy a surprise for Joe. But, sooner or later, the facts will hold sway. What would provide a more adequate solution to need conflicts is some sort of social system, some set of group rules which will spell out requirements. But, to appreciate group rules requires a recognition of a unit or force which is not concrete in the sense of being tangible like an individual. Such a group could represent the guardian of general practices which justifies those practices or actions. When these perceptions come to a person, that person has moved to stage three, the first stage of the conventional level.

The conventional level necessitates a move from the concrete egoistic view of the pre-conventional level to a cognitive recognition of the value of a group, group practices and group rules. It also moves from an evaluation of actions in terms of consequences to an evaluation of actions in terms of how well they fulfill the expectations of a group in their own right regardless of the consequences to oneself. Kohlberg describes the conventional level in this way:

At this level, maintaining the expectations of the individual's family, group or nation is perceived as valuable in its own right, regardless of immediate or obvious consequences. The attitude is not only one of conformity to personal expectations and social order, but of loyalty to it, of actively maintaining, supporting and justifying the order and of identifying with the persons or group involved in it. This level comprises two stages: "good boy-nice girl" orientation and "law and order" orientation.[5]

The first thing to say about the perspectives characteristic of the conventional level is that they involve a valuing of a group and the feeling of belonging to a group in a way that indicates a real socialization which is more than simply the pragmatic backscatching we saw in stage two. One's perspective of stage two was to see others in the same boat as himself. In normal development this leads to a realization that the rules of a group or society might be the results of these people attempting to live in harmony, and to the realization that living in harmony is a pleasurable experience. However, it is an experience which involves some self-sacrifice on the part of all involved in the group. There ought to be some guarantee that if I scratch your back, you'll scratch mine, but that guarantee seems to entail gratitude. If one lives in a family where there is love and understanding, there will be plenty of examples of one person or another performing an action that is pleasant for me but brings him no discernible reward.

At this transition stage the individual begins to realize that the esteem and approval of others is becoming more important than concrete rewards but that this esteem and approval only come if one is willing to pitch in and do one's share. Also at this stage we find individuals who need a sense of self-worth. Belonging to a group where one is important reinforces one's notion of self-worth. It is not far-fetched to note that the kind of satisfaction that is anticipated from belonging to a group and from group loyalty is reflected well in the lyrics of the popular song of a few years ago: "People who need people are the luckiest people in the world."

But this perspective and affective tone of the person at level two must be cognitively explained. The most important cognitive determinant in moving to the conventional level seems to be what is called the ability to "roll-take" or, more commonly, to "emphathize." Such an ability is the ability to put oneself in the mind and place of another, to see things from his point of view. This ability is the cognitive condition which allows a person at the conventional level to recognize the limits and unsatisfactoriness of egoism and to see the need for group cooperation.

The example of Joe and his father will help to illustrate how this occurs. Joe's father, it will be remembered, wants Joe's money, and if Joe is at stage two this is bad because Joe will not achieve the pleasure he anticipated. Joe is capable of seeing things from his father's point of view and of realizing that if the money can bring him pleasure it can bring his father pleasure too. But who has the right to the money? Joe's father, because he is more powerful, or Joe, because he has earned it? In stage one the authority of the father would have held sway as the reason, but in stage two Joe has the right because he is not overawed by power and thinks of his own pleasure. Still if pleasure is good for Joe it is good for his father. Given two people with a claim to money which will bring them both pleasure, how do we resolve the question of who has the right to it? If there were a system of rules governing such social relations, they could resolve it. At this point, some sort of social system is required, since the concrete consequences are not sufficient considerations for resolving the issue.

Presumably some sort of reasoning like the following takes place, at least implicitly in the mind of the person moving from stage two to stage three: If we are all people who have the same sorts of desires and feelings, and if there is some good thing that would bring two or more people pleasure, and if only one of them can have it, we need some sort of social system to decide. An issue like this will raise cognitive disequilibrium in a stage two person. Such a person, however, can recognize the existence of groups and the roles in groups which have their respective rights and obligations. The existence of groups like the family seems to determine the proper relationships between individuals, not simply based on desires and feelings but on some sort of social structure. A father should not be like a brother. One might expect a brother to take Joe's money, but a father? The proper role of a father does not allow the sort of self-interest that Joe's father is manifesting. In some such way as this, group roles are seen to be the determiners of right and wrong.

Kohlberg defines the stage three orientation this way: "The interpersonal concordance of 'good boy—nice girl' orientation. Good behavior is that which pleases or helps others and is approved by them. There is much conformity to stereotypical images of what is majority or 'natural' behavior. Behavior is frequently judged by intention. 'He means well' becomes important for the first time. One earns approval by being 'nice.' "[6]

Stage three orientation then concentrates on thinking that self-sacrifice is the basic determinant of good and bad, and that because self-sacrifice is what makes groups succeed, and groups are now seen as necessary, both cognitively and affectively, self-sacrifice is also necessary. However, it would be a mistake to think that the stage two egoism is totally gone. It has not been completely dissipated. Rather what occurs in the transition from stage two to stage three is a substitution of a less concrete form of pleasure, "the approval of others" for the more concrete immediate goods that gave pleasure before. There seems to be a switch from striving for physical pleasure to striving for the psychological pleasure which comes through social approval. Thus one recognizes that being helpful to others and being kind and considerate are the ways the authorities have indicated that such approval, and its consequent good feeling, will come. Since one is still dependent on authority, it will be the stereotyped expectations of behavior that will indicate what good behavior is.[7]

Beyond this orientation, however, there is, as Kohlberg notes, the judging of another's actions by intention, by an appeal to "He means well." It is instructive to see how this also flows out of the cognitive disequilibrium created for the stage two person. As a child grows he is very often struck by two things. Sometimes he does something that he thinks will please an adult, only to have the action cause anger and upset in the adults. Recall the Piaget example of the boy filling his father's pen. At other times a child does something with the best intentions in the world, only to have them come out all wrong. Imagine a child rearranging his room and turning it into a decorator's nightmare. This kind of experience should, sooner or later, indicate to the child that an action can't simply be judged by its consequences. He thinks that some merit or reward or recognition ought to be given for his good intentions. Something should have worked, but it did not. This action should have brought pleasure, but it did not. Consequences of actions, then, cannot be the sole criterion of good or bad. It is important to consider a person's motives in evaluating his actions.

An eighth grade girl whom we interviewed thought that the judge should be lenient with Heinz because he stole the drug for the love of his wife. A good husband might have to do the "wrong" thing because that was his role as a good husband. Here clearly the priority in judging an action was the intention rather than the consequences of the action. In these ways then, stage three thinking is superior to stage two thinking. It has a wider view of society, and a better understanding of the purpose of rules and roles. Further it allows one to distinguish between an action, its consequences, and the intention of the person performing the action. At this stage the group seems to be a natural entity, and the rules of the group are rules which set up pre-determined roles which the individual members fill in order to bring about harmony. To be good is to fit into one's slot. The egocentric individual of stage two has become socialized in his cognitive outlook.

For some, it is possible to think back on that time of life of early adolescence and remember the positive joy that came from belonging, from having a function. That joy was so large that it was enough to impel one to gladly sacrifice one's life for the group or the community he held most dear, if only he were asked. No pain was too great, no sacrifice too large to perform for the sake of the group. All one needed was to have his role defined and his performance in that role approved. But there is a difficulty in this stage. The ideals are naive and stereotyped. What does one do with conflicting roles demanding opposite courses of action? What response is to be given to the question of whether Heinz should be sentenced by the judge? Heinz was carrying out the role of a good husband. He was good. But the judge has a role to play too. Does not the role of the judge demand that he sentence Heinz? But how can he if Heinz was carrying out his role as a concerned husband? This type of perplexity will disturb the equilibrium and demand a less naive standard of moral response, a more adequate cognitive response. That standard will be found in stage four.

Another problem with stage three thinking might arise if one experiences people who are not playing their proper role. Take the case of Joe and his father. A good father would not ask for the money. But he did, and a good son should give his father what he asks for. When faced with the problem of whether Joe should give his father the money, our eighth grade girl hesitated and then responded, "Well, it would be nice. A nice son would do that. Still, a nice father shouldn't have asked. But perhaps the father had good reasons for asking." The girl was having a difficult time imagining that a father could do such a thing without a reason.

Finally, there is yet another difficulty. The stage three individual presumably will experience different groups with conflicting group expectations. If one is disturbed by such conflicts, he or she will again go in search of a more adequate cognitive solution which will afford a way of adjudicating conflicting groups and which will afford rules by which to justify individual behavior. Here develops the most abstract conception available so far, the concept of a set of rules for society as a whole, a moral law which governs all men and justifies or condemns existing groups or institutions. The abstract concept of the moral law is devised, and one has reached the highest and most adequate concept at the conventional level, and a type of reasoning which Kohlberg designates as stage four. Still, before moving to a consideration of stage four, let us talk about the pragmatics involved in dealing with people at stage three.

It ought to be obvious that at this stage the subjects will be operating out of group loyalty. Think of all the children in early adolescence who will do anything to be helpful and nice. Think of how much they admire heroes or idols. To get a stage three person to respond, one can appeal to a group loyalty and approve of what he is doing. Yet, there is a difficulty present for those working with people at stage three. To which group is the person being loyal? It will be a group where one feels accepted and to which one has an affinity. A person at stage three may affiliate with a group that the person's parents, school, or society does not approve. It is not requisite that the development of group identity be an identifying with church, state, or family. It might be identification with a peer group. Egoism is not far behind, and the approval of a group is a necessary factor in achieving stage three. Consequently, if a person in developing receives little or no approval at home or school, then he or she will identify more and more with his or her peers. That community's values then will take precedence over those of the family or school.

Stage three, then, is idealistic in that it holds out models and stereotypes to be emulated, and it is altruistic in that service to a community or group is more important than service to oneself. However, one does not stop at stage three. As we mentioned, the stage three person became aware of the facts that roles conflict, that people do not live up to their roles, and, finally, that society is made up of all sorts of different groups whose goals and values conflict. The unreliability of people and the conflict of groups and the tug of different groups leave the person in disequilibrium. How are these conflicts to be resolved? When a stage three person sees an overarching social order which provides laws and rules that address the rights of all and which adjudicates the conflicts of individual and group interests, a beginning is made.

What started as a concrete identification with a group or groups yields to an identifying with one system which is seen as overarching and adequate. Particular rules for particular groups are not enough. We need rules to define the place for groups themselves in the social order. Hence, we need laws for society.

Kohlberg calls stage four orientation the "Law and Order Orientation." At this stage, there is an "orientation toward authority, fixed rules and the maintenance of the social order. Right behavior consists in doing one's duty, showing respect for authority and maintaining the given social order for its own sake."[8] The person thus "orients to society as a system of fixed rule, law and authority with the prospect of any deviation from rules as leading to social chaos."[9]

A person with a developed abstractive ability now does not simply see himself as a member of a specific group or of specific groups, but as a "generalized member of society."[10] Obviously, the most adequate system cognitively would be a system which guarantees order, with general moral terms or moral principles.

Group loyalty is not enough, personal relations are not enough, good intentions are not enough. One must abide by the rule of the law. Otherwise, society and the social order crumble. Right behavior consists in doing one's duty, which Kohlberg sees as responsibilities awarded to individuals by the social order. A person who has a stage four orientation can sympathize with a person who breaks a law, but this sympathy will be overriden by a concern to uphold the social order which requires a strict adherence to rules and proper authority.

To put it simply, there is a passage from a stage three concern for a group and the success of the group to a more abstract concern for the law, so that one's obligation to the law overrides one's obligations of loyalty to one's friends and groups. A person at stage four then wll appear as a passionate devotee of the law.

This stage is the highest stage of moral reasoning before the level of principled thinking and could very well be the stage of the majority of adults. It is a stage of reverence for the law and legitimate authority, because the law is seen as the ultimate guarantee of peace, order and individual's rights. It is a stage which insists that no man is above the law, that no group is above the law.

Judge Gerhard Gesell's charge to the jurors in the trial of John Ehrlichman might be viewed as a typical statement which would appeal to stage four reasoning. Gessell remarked, "An individual cannot escape criminal liability simply because he sincerely but incorrectly believes that his acts are justified in the name of patriotism, of national security, or the need to create a favorable press image, or that his superiors had the power to suspend without a warrant the protections of the Fourth Amendment."[11] Gesell was reminding Ehrlichman that loyalty to a man or president is not a sufficient reason to justify violating the law.

Whereas in stage three there is an attachment to persons, an appreciation of their motives, and a strong sense of loyalty, which makes one willing to overlook infractions, in stage four the law is seen as the ultimate guarantee of people's rights because it is the ultimate guarantee of social order. One is not ready and willing to overlook people's misguided loyalties or good intentions if these endanger the social order. This may make well-meaning people who are stage four oriented seem at times almost callous in their disregard for individuals when these individuals violate the law. Since a stage four person would think that in the case of Heinz the judge has a definite responsibility to sentence him in some way or other, we might think him callous. However, lest we, in some sort of humanitarian self-delusion, think that this is a lower stage of reasoning than stage three, let us remember our own feelings in the case of Watergate. If someone thought that the defendants should get off scot free, that the laws need not be applied in the case of some defendants, let us remember the outcries when Richard Kliendienst was given such a light sentence. The chief reaction was to the impropriety of the judge's remarking on how well-intentioned a fellow Kliendienst was.

Think of how many ways we support stage four reasoning. Think of the demands made on persons to report infractions on the part of their best friends if these friends violated an honor system. Note the existence of demands by legal groups that members report illegal violations of others even if these are violations performed by their closest associates. There is no egoism in this kind of respect for the law. There is no promise of reward, only the expectation of the maintenance of one's duty. Not even the approval of the group is looked for in this situation. Indeed, the real hero of stage four is he who upholds the law even when all around are cursing him for doing it. Why? Because in the long run he will be chief contributor to the social order.

It seems clear that an overarching law which adjudicates rival claims between persons and groups is a much more adequate basis for moral judgment than the haphazard sentimentalism and favoritism that can arise from stage three reasoning. Still, all in all, at stage four there is a distinction to be made. One may be tempted to talk about "the law" and may even codify it. But the question is: Which law and which authority? Early in stage four the person will assume that just as there was authority in the individual group so there is authority for society as a whole. Yet, there is a disagreement about which laws are part of "the law" and which authority is "the authority." Consequently, there is yet another move and a modification of stage four. Whereas originally there is orientation to the law, now there is orientation to what is behind the rules. Kohlberg calls this stage "Four B."

Stage Four B has three possible orientations to what is behind the rules:

(a) "The purpose of the law and rules in terms of utility or the welfare of the majority or of others." Laws and rules are viewed as being for the sake of the common good. To preserve and protect the common good is all-important. Hence, if a particular rule violates the common good, it is to be abandoned or reformed, for it is an unjust rule. This utility then gives the ground out of which the laws spring.

(b) One can see the laws as being based on "the wishes, agreement, and viewpoint of the majority." The majority rules. Here the laws are seen as the reflection of the views of the majority.

(c) Or, one can see "the moral law" as the consensus of society's norms and beliefs which: (1) may conflict with legal or positive law at particular points, and (2) may go beyond conventional role-obligations."[12]

In this view then, the law is not simply a table of do's or don'ts, but is some ordering principle that resides behind the do's and don'ts. An example to distinguish Four A thinking from Four B thinking may be helpful. Some subjects at stage Four A who are faced with the Heinz dilemma will respond to the effect that, although they understand and sympathize with Heinz' plight, stealing is wrong and cannot be condoned, for to condone it in even one instance is an invitation to chaos and anarchy. A stage Four B person however, while admitting that it is against the law to steal, might justify Heinz' taking of the drug, since obviously the rule against stealing merely reflects a practice which generally leads to the welfare of the majority, or is generally a rule which reflects the will of the majority, even though in this specific instance the rule might thwart the presumed will of the majority.

The chief point about stage four, however, is that the person relates to the law as something given which commands his respect and obedience, as well as the respect and obedience of all people. It is society's law, and as a member of society the person comes under the law.

Yet, in Kohlberg's theory, there are still two stages which are higher, in a principled or post-conventional level. Now, whereas movement through the first four stages was characterized by a more adequate perception of what the social system is, this is not the case in the movement from stage four to five, or from the conventional level. Principled thinking, according to Kohlberg, does not involve a more adequate perception of what the social system is: rather it involves "a postulation of principles to which the society and the self *ought* to be committed."[13] Principled thinking involves a move to moral theory, by which is meant not only a concern for justifying particular laws or rules, but a concern for discovering the most basic principles from which all laws are derived.

At some time a person may come to realize that the order our society approves may not be the best possible order, or that other societies have other systems. At that point, the question can arise whether the system our society commits itself to is the *best* possible system. For example, one can accept the notion of private property as a given order, but ask, say, from a Marxist point of view whether such a system is really the most desirable. Basically, what occurs in the movement from the conventional view is a questioning of "society's view," a questioning of the received traditions and standards of the society in general. This amounts to an orientation which is an "outside of society perspective," a standpoint of some natural self which allows one to look at any system or society including one's own as a fact which may or may not live up to an ideal order. Reason is the basis of judging what the ideal is toward which societies ought to strive. The principles which reason furnishes are the basis of ethical theory. Such a state is autonomous, for one is freed from society's views, and this autonomy, for Kohlberg, is the most adequate ethical or moral posture.

Kohlberg, joining with most contemporary ethical theorists, insists, as they do, on one criterion of moral maturity that is lacking in the four stages which comprise the pre-conventional and conventional level. That criterion is autonomy in judgment. What autonomy in judgment means for Kohlberg is simply making up one's mind for oneself about what is right and wrong. We have alluded to this in the introduction when we cited the example of the girl of twenty-eight who warded off the advances toward sex by appealing to the fact that her mother told her it was wrong.

Basically, what the point comes down to is this. If a person spends his whole life doing what he has been told to do by authority, merely because of fear of authority (stage one), or because it will bring him pleasure (stage two), or because it is expected by the group (stage three), or because that is the law, (stage four), he has never really made moral decisions which are his *own* moral decisions. He may be acting in accord with laws, but is he accepting these laws because he is conditioned to accept them, or because he has chosen them as the most ideal? If I do something my father approves of without examining whether it is acceptable, I am merely following my father's principles, not my own. One must be one's own person, so to speak, in order to mature fully. One must develop one's own principles of judgment and action. It will not do merely to follow what one has been told. Thus, Kohlberg describes the post-conventional, autonomous, or principled level as one where there is a "clear effort to define moral values and principles which have validity and application apart from the authority of the groups or persons holding these principles and apart from the individual's own identification with these groups."[14] At a principled level then, the individual thinks for himself, and if he is to come to grips with a group he identifies with, he must do so by himself, independently of others in authority. He must accept a group only insofar as he in his own conscience can live with it. No group mind may supplant his own conscience.

Earlier in his research, Kohlberg was inclined to think that students reached these principled levels of thought at about the time they were reaching the end of high school. Further studies on his subjects, however, over a long period of time (some of the subjects are now reaching their late thirties), convinced Kohlberg that there was a transitional stage (resembling stage two) between the conventional and post-conventional levels. He called it stage four and one-half, and in many ways it is a stage describing the necessary conditions which must be met if one is to achieve autonomy. The stage is characterized by (1) skepticism, (2) egoism, and (3) relativism.

An analogy might help to understand how one reaches this "outside society perspective," this standpoint of some natural self. Imagine that there is a primitive society without contact with the outside world, since the group is completely surrounded by mountains and other societies are inaccessible for all practical purposes. We need very little anthropological knowledge to realize that this group will be highly organized according to a system of rules and taboos. These rules will be enforced with sanctions, either natural or conventional. Suppose one of the rules is to attend a certain tribal ritual at specified periods of time. Suppose also that the tribe believes (with no basis in fact) that not attending the ritual makes a member infectious to the other members, and thus they ostracize such an offender from the group for a period of a month, thereby never verifying the existence of the mysterious infectious powers. Now, suppose one of the members of the tribe, having violated the taboo, is ostracized. While being ostracized, he climbs up the mountain and discovers a path to another valley. Going down he encounters a new tribe with practices he has never seen before. They require no mandatory attendance at rituals and do not end up being infected by him. They perform practices which are forbidden in his tribe while outlawing practices which are perfectly normal for his tribe. Now, if he left his own valley absolutely convinced that the rules of his tribe were universal, that is, were the best rules for society (and why should he not assume that, since he had encountered no other sets of rules?), what would this experience do to him? It would make him aware of the fact that not everything he thought to be the law was necessarily the law. He would be exposed to other ways of doing things. These other ways did not lead to chaos. Would he not then become skeptical of the correctness of his own tribe's rules? Would he not also become skeptical of the correctness of the foreign tribe's rules? Would he not begin to wonder about the best or ideal ways of behaving? The magical hold that his picture of the proper order of things had over him would be broken, unless, of course, he viewed these strange people as monsters.

Let us suppose, further, that he left that valley to return home to enlighten his people as to their stupidity in some matters, but took a different passage and encountered yet another tribe with other practices and rules. If he were bright enough and tolerant enough, would he not begin to view the rules of each society as relative to the beliefs and needs of that society? Would not a relativism begin to develop?

But what about the egoism? Let us follow him further. After a long odyssey, let him finally return to his native tribe. He has marvels to relate. He must tell the authorities that some of their practices are wasteful, that there are better ways of doing some things, and that some practices might be downright dangerous. How would he be accepted by the tribal chiefs, the authorities who were the interpreters of the received law which was absolute for all men? He would, needless to say, probably be punished as a harmful maverick. Thus, two things happen to our primitive wanderer: First, he is intellectually disillusioned about beliefs he held sacred. Now, on his return, he is alienated from the tribe because of these beliefs. This must have an effect on his emotional attachment to the group. He becomes intellectually and emotionally isolated. He needs society, he loves his home, but he is cut off from it because of an intellectual awakening. He sees his tribe's rules no longer as special, but as ranging alongside the rules of every other tribe. They no longer give him comfort and intellectual assurance that he is on the right way. He must think for himself, for there is no one to guide him. Having been forced out of the contentment of certitude and ease of practice in the rules of the community, he has nowhere to turn for comfort and solace. He may become embittered and cynical about society, thus turning wholly inward. This characterizes the new egoism.

That, I think, gives a picture of the structural outlook characteristic of stage four and one-half. Is there not a great deal of similarity between our imagined voyager and our college youth? Prospective college students leave an organized community where they have grown up and accustomed themselves to the expectations of parents, peers and teachers, and enter a new community where there are few, if any, rules or regulations, and where presentations by teachers are painfully objective and neutral. All sides of the issue are given. The flaws in their picture of the ordered universe are exposed as mercilessly as the flaws in every other picture of an ordered universe. The intellectual and affective stability that have surrounded the child up to late adolescence is shattered. A serious identity crisis develops. Things are not as he thought they were. His authority figures have no more hold. Where will he go to find his values? Our college students are uprooted from their comfortable secure world and thrust into an atmosphere where there are few answers and mostly questions, and where they must live with people whose life styles need not resemble theirs at all. The egoism and self-concern at this stage is not stage two egoism of self-interest; it is a desperate egoism of isolation, of being alienated from society, and earnestly yearning for incorporation into a newly meaningful society. The love of order has not disappeared; it just seems to have been cynically betrayed. Societies are seen as full of sham and hypocrisy, for they claim to know what they do not and to provide comfort which they cannot.

Society begins to look like the society of the egoist described in Plato's *Republic* (Bk. II) by Glaucon. According to Glaucon's account, men have only come together out of self-interest, to protect themselves. The really wise man is the one who sees through the sham of altruistic demands and takes what he can get, using society and conforming to it only insofar as that is necessary to promote his own interest. Men are basically selfish, and what keeps most of them in place is fear and timidity. This is a classic egoistic view. It promotes self-indulgence, and lampoons altruism and concern for others as stupidity.

Now, if our college student feels thus betrayed by his society, by the groups to whom he felt loyal, where is he to turn? He could follow the cynical egoism related above, or he could search around for meaningful relationships with other people. One cannot live alone very well, so one must pick up the pieces and attempt to build a new society with its own order, or refashion the old according to new ideals. I had often thought that love among the young was a hopelessly romantic affair, based on dreams and wishes of eternal bliss. How else explain the absolute dependence and constant togetherness of young lovers? However, if one adopts a Kohlbergian framework, one can look at this young love as much more. One can see it as a reaching out for another, coupled with a desperate hope that there are good relationships that can be achieved. If there are, then society may be a worthwhile thing. Thus, young love may be the first venture of the person alienated from his old traditions and values and beliefs learned in the society he has left, to build a new society. It is a positive affirmation of the anti-egoistic tendency that will propel him to a new level of moral development.

Obviously, not all individuals go through such a drastic disillusionment with the society that nurtured them. One could hazard a guess that the rejection of society's laws are made piecemeal. Nevertheless, even a rejection of a single law that once was believed as fixed and given involves a "natural man standpoint." That law, and eventually other laws too, may be examined by ideals forged by reason.

In detailing stages five and six, Kohlberg describes two different ways of getting at those ideals or principles by virtue of which we judge the existing social order. Stage five is the social contract legalistic orientation. Let me cite Kohlberg's full description:

> The social contract legalistic orientation. Generally with utilitarian overtones. Right action tends to be defined in terms of general individual rights and in terms of standards which have been critically examined and agreed upon by the whole society. There is a clear awareness of the relativism of personal values and opinions and a corresponding emphasis upon procedural rules for reaching consensus. Aside from what is con-

stitutionally and democratically agreed upon, the right is a matter of personal values and opinion. The result is an emphasis upon the legal point of view, but with an emphasis upon the possibility of changing law in terms of rational consideration of social utility (rather than rigidly maintaining it in terms of Stage Four law and order). Outside the legal realm, free agreement and contract is the binding element of obligation. This is the "official" morality of the American government and Constitution.[15]

Stage five follows logically upon four and one-half. If a person thinks societies are relative to the people living in them, he will then be tempted to think they are set up in some sort of legalistic way, perhaps by a social contract. But they must be set up so that they make sense. Having been a skeptic, he thinks that most moral judgments are a matter of personal opinion or a reflection of a majority's will. But what one group holds as right, another will not. How is one to adjudicate the differences? Our stage five person, being disillusioned with a stage four certitude that held a fixed order, knows no authority to adjudicate. Hence, rational considerations of social utility, democratically agreed upon and subject to review and reform, seem to be the best answer. (Social utility here means the greatest good for the greatest number, the common good, the general welfare or the public interest.)

At stage five, one also distinguishes between areas of personal freedom and areas which concern the public good. In the former areas, a person is entitled to his own beliefs, practices and opinions, as long as he does not hurt anyone else. Where his practices *do* affect the lives of others, these practices can be legislated, indeed *need* to be legislated.

As we can see, the major difference between stage four and five is the difference in the belief of the fixity or "givenness" of law and the difference in the belief of the existence of an authority to deliver or promulgate the laws. Whereas in stage four the law is something given, something fixed, which gives order to society, stage five sees the law as something which is the creation of men who tried to frame laws on the basis of what they saw as the common good. Law is man's own invention, democratically designed to meet man's needs.

The experiences of four and one-half allowed the individual to see different systems of laws, and this led to a doubting of any fixed system. It led to the belief that there are a variety of possible orders and that existent systems depend on the needs, beliefs and environments of the peoples involved. This leads to a denial of the pre-existence of a universal system of laws which all men should abide by. The law came from men trying to co-exist. Hence, law is man's creation and man need not be an idolater of the law.

It ought to be clear, then, that a stage five person, by being in a position to challenge and critically examine a law, is in a very important sense free of the law until he decides it is rational, and consequently decides to subject himself to it. A classic statement of a post-conventional level type made to a stage four type is that of Jesus when he reminds the legalistic Pharisees that "the sabbath is made for man, not man for the sabbath." There was a reason for the law—to aid man. That is the justification of any law. But when positively made law interferes with the person it is meant to aid, it becomes self-defeating.

It is important to note that stage five thinking, although critical, is not arbitrary. One's rejection of existing law and proposals of new laws must be subject to rational considerations and critiques. If they are detrimental to the common good they can be jettisoned, but they cannot be jettisoned simply because they do not serve one's self-interest (stage two thinking) or because they don't meet one's own ideals (stage three thinking). Society is seen as absolutely essential, and its preservation is seen to rest on a critical appraisal of its rules and practices.

One is tempted at this point to leave off the discussion of Kohlberg's stages for several reasons. It will be remembered that one cannot grasp a level of reasoning more than one above one's own. My belief is that a great segment of society is probably located at the fourth stage or in the transitional stage of four and one-half. So for most of us, if there is a highest stage, it might be quite difficult to comprehend. Further, Kohlberg himself admits that the interview data is quite sparse, and to explain stage six he usually turns to examples of literature or words of contemporary heroes, such as Gandhi or Martin Luther King. For example, he cites the following passage from King's notes from a Birmingham jail as an example of stage six reasoning. "One may well ask, 'How can you advocate breaking some laws and obeying others?' The answer lies in the fact that there are two types of laws, just and unjust. One has not only a legal but a moral responsibility to obey just laws. One has a moral responsibility to disobey unjust laws. Any law that uplifts human personality is just, any law that degrades human personality is unjust. An unjust law is a code that a numerical or power majority group compels a minority group to obey but does not make binding on itself. This is difference made legal."[16]

This is indeed principled thinking. But what in it makes it stage six? What makes it a reasoning higher and better than stage five reasoning? What makes it cognitively more adequate?

I submit that this is a very difficult issue and one that Kohlberg has not succeeded in resolving in his own mind. One sign of this irresolution is his recent theorizing about a stage seven.[17] But it would be presumptuous to blame the fuzziness about the highest stages of reasoning on Kohlberg alone. What happens is that in reaching the highest stages of development we are probably leaving the majority of men behind. This makes interview data almost inaccessible. What we are forced to do, then, is to leave considerations of data behind and venture into philosophical speculation. We then begin to philosophize about possible stages rather than talk about actual ones. For these reasons it seems to me that discussion of the post-conventional level is much more problematic than discussion of the first two levels. In the upper level, we are dealing more with theoretical possibilities than with existent actualities.

Despite these reservations and difficulties, let us look at stage six which Kohlberg describes as the "universal ethical principle orientation." This, presumably, is the highest level of development in moral reasoning. "Right," according to Kohlberg, "is defined by the decision of conscience in accord with self-chosen ethical principles appealing to logical comprehensiveness, universality and consistency. These principles are abstract and ethical (the golden rule, the categorical imperative) and are not concrete moral rules like the ten commandments. At heart, these are universal principles of justice, of the reciprocity and equality of human rights, and of respect for the dignity of human beings as individual persons."[18]

Perhaps we can illustrate stage six by a comparison with stage five. Since, presumably, stage five requires also "a decision of conscience in accord with self-chosen ethical principles," meaning that it is on the principled, autonomous, post-conventional level, the difference between five and six must be in the appeal. Whereas stage five thinking appeals to social utility—that is, to those consequences of actions which bring about the general welfare—stage six thinking appeals to logical comprehensiveness, universality, and consistency. Now, what does that mean? On first reading, it appears that stage six thinking is concerned with the logic of moral reasoning. But one need not be a principled thinker to be concerned with that; one need only take a course in elementary logic and run arguments through a validity proof.

However, to any student of ethical theory it calls to mind the fundamental difference between the ethical theories of John Stuart Mill and Immanuel Kant. Whereas Mill held that the value of any action lay in the worthwhile consequences it produced, Kant thought that the worth of an action lay in the law or maxim under which it was performed. Thus, if I gave alms for a tax write-off, that was prudent, but not morally virtuous. If, however, I gave alms out of a belief that I had a duty to help those less fortunate, then that was morally virtuous. The consequences are the same— the poor get alms—but from Kant's point of view the latter case showed the higher motivation. Now, for Kant, every action has a motivation, that is, it is performed under some rationale. But all rationales are not equally good. Thus he devised a test of these rationales which checked their comprehensiveness, universality and consistency. The test was derived from what Kant called the categorical imperative, which enjoins us to act only on that maxim (rational reason) which you can will to become universal law. Thus, if you are willing to have everyone adopt your reason for doing something, you have a genuinely universal, comprehensive and consistent rule.

Recent ethical theory has alluded to the Gospel of Matthew for an example. There, B owes A a large sum of money. A forgives the debt. However, C owes B a lesser sum of money, which B will not forgive. B is inconsistent, for if he ruled that C ought to pay his debts to B, then B ought to pay his debts to A, or if A ought to forgive his debts to B then B ought to forgive his debts to C. If this sounds like "do unto others as you would have them do unto you," the golden rule, it *is* very close to that, and Kant's test is likewise very similar. However, notice that in deciding that B did wrong, there was no consideration of social utility. Suppose B was a desperately poor man, partly because he had lent his money to C. Suppose further that C did not need the money, whereas B did. An argument could be generated that from the point of view of social utility what was done by B was proper. Yet, Kant does not consider the consequences of the action. Whether that reflects a higher level of moral reasoning we leave to the reader to decide.

The moral convictions that the examples of A, B and C bring to light are the convictions of equality. No man has special rights to special treatment under the law. Each man, as a man, counts as much as every other. That is why Kant will not consider circumstances like those where B is poorer than C. Further, Kant thinks his universalizing test (How would it be if everyone did that? How would it be if A did to B what B did to C?) yields another version of the categorical imperative: "Act so as to treat any rational being as an end-in-himself and never merely as a means." Herein lies one of the most profound statements of the dignity of man. Every man is an end-in-himself, has dignity as a human being, and it degrades that dignity to treat him as a means. For example, it is unjustifiable to blackmail a person for money even if that money were to be used for a life-saving project guaranteed of success and even if the person could afford it. It is unjustifiable because it used the person with money merely as an instrument.

These seem to be the sort of considerations which Kohlberg has in mind when he says that the principles appealed to in stage six are "universal principles of justice, of the reciprocity and equality of human rights, and of respect for the dignity of human beings as individual persons." But let us give a final example to try to sharpen our perception of what is involved in a stage six orientation. We already cited Martin Luther King's notes from a Birmingham jail as an example of stage six thinking. But King admits that he must answer the question "How can you advocate breaking some laws and obeying others?" Could not someone ask, legitimately, how this advocacy toward breaking laws is any different than the advocacy of breaking laws on the part of the Watergate defendants? Is there a double standard here? Pick your good guys and put them at stage six, and your bad guys and put them at a stage two or three or four? I think not, and I think we can point out the difference.

Remember that King offered as a maxim "Disobey unjust laws" and went on to define an unjust law as a "code that a numerical or power majority group compels a minority group to obey, but does not make binding on itself." Was it not the case that the Watergate defendants failed to make all laws binding on themselves? If so, didn't they then, in effect, set up a higher law for themselves, one which allowed them to use their own discretion as to which actions were right and proper for them, while insisting that such actions were not right and proper for others? Did not their actions under their higher law allow them to use others as means to their own ends, and isn't this a law that degrades human dignity and can in no way be universalized? King, however, calls for universally applicable laws and would revoke as unjust those which are not universally applicable. That, then, is the difference between principled moral judgment and arbitrary moral action.

One more expository comment. When Kohlberg says that these principles are "not concrete moral rules like the ten commandments," I think he has in mind their abstract nature. It would follow from Kant's injunction never to treat others merely as means that we ought not to kill, steal, lie, etc. The ten commandments are specific moral rules. *Principles* are overarching formulas which are meant to be applied. There are memorable ones: Christ's law of love, Augustine's "Love and do what you will," etc. They don't tell one specifically how to act in this or that case.

As we said, Kohlberg mentions some specific examples of stage six individuals. They seem to be persons who are motivated by an extreme sensitivity to and concern for others. His list includes Martin Luther King and Mahatma Gandhi. We could add Christ, Buddha, St. Paul, St. Francis of Assisi, etc. The identifying factor is high principle that may run counter to established conventions, certainly not egoistic, but, on the contrary, concerned with the dignity of others. This is the stage of moral heroes.

This sketchy outline of stage six then brings us to the end of our journey through Kohlberg's stages.

III
Moral Development
from a Christian Perspective

Up to this point, we have presented the theories of Piaget and Kohlberg, with little or no comment on the relevance of their theories to Christian moral development. What we will do now is reflect on what impact these theories have on Christian morality.

First, however, let us consider the notion of Christian morality, particularly from the point of view of the question: Is there a morality which *is* specifically Christian? This is a very significant question. To map out the various positions and arguments in support of alternative answers would require a book in itself. We will not do that, but will simply mention some obvious difficulties raised by those who claim there is no specifically Christian morality as well as indicate some considerations to support a claim that there is.

First the difficulties. Every so often, as I did a few weeks ago, I find myself approving a course of action by saying, "That is a very Christian thing to do." If one lived in a self-sustaining ghetto community where there were only Christians, that kind of utterance would cause no disturbance. However, I live and work in a community where there are Christians, Jews, Moslems, atheists, agnostics, etc. It is quite self-righteous to say to a Moslem, for instance, that he did a Christian thing, particularly when that Moslem snaps back, "It's a Moslem thing, too." We are being told, in no uncertain terms, that Christians do not have a corner on correct behavior, that, believe it or not, other people try to live decent up-standing lives.

I can remember attending a Christian-Marxist dialogue with the atheist-communist Herbert Aptheker in which he was asked, "Why, if you don't believe in God, do you devote yourself to your cause so faithfully and persistently?" Aptheker smiled benignly, and in a calm soft voice responded in words to this effect: "Why? Because my cause is the service of my fellow man, and true happiness is found in serving one's fellow man." He then went on to remind the audience that this had been the great message of all organized religions.

The problem Aptheker's comment raises is the very real question: "If an avowed atheist can arrive at love of one's fellow man as the foremost moral ideal, what *need* do we have of a religiously based morality—specifically a Christian morality?

William Frankenna, a committed Calvinist and highly respected ethical philosopher, states in his book *Ethics:* "One needs to distinguish the moral point of view from the religious point of view. Ethics has its own principles quite distinct from religion."[1]

Given positions like Aptheker's and Frankenna's, does it follow that religious belief and God are irrelevant to ethics? I certainly do not think so, and will try to indicate in what ways they are relevant. Still, we should note that for some there is a distinct difference between a moral and a religious point of view. Such a recognition will prevent us from too facile a conjoining of religion and morality and remind us, as Christians that we do not have the corner on the truth about moral issues. Therefore, we ought not to be over-bearing or self-righteous in asserting that because we are "Catholic" or "Christian" or the "people of God" we are automatically plugged in to some supernatural source of principles or rules, or that we are plugged directly into God and hence guaranteed the truth of our position.

How is God or religion relevant to ethics? One way which seems clear is that a belief in a religion has a theoretical and a practical aspect. Theoretically it gives one a world perspective, a metaphysical view of man and his relation to a transcendent being. But if such a metaphysical view is religious, it will have existential impact, and will result in practical judgments and actions.

Let me give a concrete example: A man slapped in the face may be "resigned" or may have "capitulated." Resignation is a different description of an action that can also be called "capitulation." Whether a man is resigned or capitulating depends on the disposition of the man, and the disposition in turn depends on his beliefs about the ends and nature of man. One can "resign" oneself to difficulties in life because they are seen as manifesting the will of God. Marxists, however, see such passivity as "capitulation" and warn that one can be lulled by the opium of the people (religion). Thus, Marxists see clearly that religious reasons lead to certain preferences of moral ends, because these reasons reflect a view or perspective of man's relation to the universe, other men, and a transcendent being.

Thus, although we can divorce theoretical ethical concerns from practical actions for the sake of discussion, we cannot divorce existential beliefs from practical action in real life. Thus it seems that we *can* assert that there is a religious morality when there are religious reasons informing our practical judgments and actions, religious reasons being those which are informed by a religious world view, which will perforce lead to certain preferences of moral ends.

Now, presumably, Christians believe that there are certain commands or ends that are God-given and are binding on a religious community. These can be specific commands to the community, such as "Keep holy the Sabbath," or general commands for all men, propagated through the community, such as "Love your neighbor."

Suppose, then, we admit that religious reasons exist, and that there is a Christian morality. One could ask a further question about whether such a community of beliefs *should* exist or whether there *ought* to be a Christian morality.

One could only think there *ought* to be if two conditions are met. First, there must be an experience of the reality of God, a sense of the holy or transcendent. Without such an experience, any religious reasons have no existential validity—they would be mere intellectual curiosities resulting in no action. Second, there must exist a belief that the ultimate power seeks the well-being of creation (a resolution of the problem of evil) and that this ultimate power relates to man, and man relates to the ultimate power.

Otherwise, even though God might exist, he would take no interest in the affairs of man, and would have no concern when man was attempting to decide what to do.

As we indicated, without such beliefs, religious reasons become a mere intellectual curiosity having no relevance to life or action. Yet, if such beliefs exist, they will have import, for one will need to question not only *what one should do*, the ethical question, but more specifically what one should do to enhance the relationship with this ultimate power.

If one were to ask at this point how all of this relates to Kohlberg, the answer would be that a Christian perspective provides a content for the formal structure that Kohlberg identified. Christianity will provide *religious reasons* for our moral beliefs.

For example, if one is at a stage where one looks for a fixed law and believes in the existence of an all-knowing, all-powerful God, that God will be the author of the law. Thus, if one is at a stage where he is responsive to fixed laws, and if he has a religious outlook, God will be seen as one of the authorities who promulgates such laws. Or, as another example, if one is at a stage where group relationships determine ideals, and is taught that the Church is a group of the chosen people of God, and that chosen people are expected to act with concern for one another, that group and its ideals will play a large role in the subject's notion of right and wrong. Thus we see that the religious beliefs about the relation of man to God and man to the Church provide a content for moral beliefs different from the content of one raised as an atheist who affiliates with no organized religious groups.

However, over and above the fact that a person's particular religious beliefs and affiliations provide content for the structures that Kohlberg has identified, it is also the case that the structures act as a filter through which these beliefs and affiliations must pass. In such a passing the beliefs and perceptions of the affiliations will be modified. For example, if a child at stage one hears you tell him that God is all-powerful, he will not get a picture of this God as concerned in his use of power and therefore provident. His stage of reasoning doesn't allow this picture to come through. Rather he will probably get a picture of God as a large man who is exceedingly strong and whose primary activity is to punish people.

In the light of this, what we propose to do is to run briefly through the stages as they might be affected by the teaching of Christian doctrine, or as the teaching of religious doctrine might be affected by the child's stage of development. I think that the process, although somewhat repetitive, given our earlier view of Kohlberg's stages, might still be illuminating in explaining some of the phenomena we encounter in our dealings with the young. It certainly ought to make us more aware of where the young are, and make us better able to communicate with them.

However, lest we sound too patronizing toward the young, we should not forget that for Kohlberg there is no such thing as necessary development. We can find *adults* at all levels of development. Chronological age is no guarantee of moral development. Thus, although we talk often about children, much of what we say can be applied to *some* adults. One does not have to search too far to find some people who do things to avoid going to hell. How often have we met someone who sighed and said, "Boy, if I didn't believe in God, I'd have a ball." God in this view is the moral enforcer and sanctioner. The good is what God allows and the bad is what God forbids. Disobedience will lead to being condemned to the everlasting fire of hell. This is a low stage of moral development, but I think the reader will have met enough people for whom it is the reason for being moral. It is fairly easy to predict the next phases of these people's lives. Either they will remain at the pre-conventional level of morality and continue to believe in God, in which case the actions of their lives will be determined by fear of this awesome God, or they will perform actions which violate the presumed "laws of God" and in order to escape the fear they will deny the existence of such a vindictive God. If they are fortunate and escape from this ego-centered pre-conventional morality, then they will either reject the moral adequacy of such a God, or move to a concept of God which can evoke feelings of gratitude and loyalty, a concept much larger than the concept of the vindictive God.

Be that as it may, it is the case that for many people, religious beliefs are inextricably bound up with moral beliefs, and it will be helpful to look at some of the relationships between them as a person moves through the developmental sequence. We turn then to an analysis of the stages as seen through the eyes of one who believes in a God and a Church. Moreover, since development into the more mature stages occurs most often in the twenties and thirties, it follows that a great many Catholic adults are still developing long past any formal education. This seems to imply that the Church should take a long look at the adult education programs, their scarcity, and their content. But more of this later. For now, let us turn to a re-examination of Kohlberg's stages.

Suppose we are dealing with a child who is at stage one, the punishment-obedient stage. Here it will be remembered that the child is inclined to judge something as good or bad depending on the painful consequences, and he is impressed with the fixed law because it comes from all-powerful authorities. To warn a child that God will punish him for doing something bad is tantamount to telling him that there are actions for which God will punish him. Too often one can hear people using God as a mental club by which they elicit obedience from children. "God won't like you if you do that." This not only reinforces stage one thinking, but it also gives an all too narrow view of God. If one wanted to keep a child at this stage, stories of hell and a vindictive God who keeps track of the smallest transgression would be an effective club. But one ought to consider what this does to the child's picture of God. At stage one, if God is the determiner of good and bad, he will invariably be viewed chiefly as a punisher. Would it not be better to appeal to a stage two level of reasoning where the good is what satisfies one's needs and occasionally the needs of others, and to portray God as one who is solicitous of the child's needs, as one who wants to make the child happy? A child at stage one understands stage two reasoning. Therefore we can move him from conceiving of God as the all-powerful punisher to conceiving of God as the Savior or Father, someone who does things to make him happy. At this stage, then, it is effective to present the laws of God as aids to his own happiness and fulfillment and to begin to develop for him a concept of God as someone to befriend, not someone to be afraid of. It would be quite effective at this stage to tell of God's sending his Son who loved all men and did kind things. Christ is precisely the kind of concrete picture of a helper which will be quite attractive, for the child at stage one can understand this kind of picture and the child at stage two is looking for someone who will instrumentally satisfy his needs. Thus to be told of Christ who came to save him, and of the kind of behavior Christ recommends to make him happy, would be an effective presentation to a child at the pre-conventional level. The notion of sacrifice will not be understood if the child is at stage one, but Christ's sacrifice will have some meaning and provide a model for the child at stage two.

It is perhaps important to note again at this point that a person cannot comprehend reasoning more than one stage higher than the stage he occupies. Too often we appeal to principles or ideals that are quite unintelligible or make recommendations that may be impossible to carry out. How many of us were taught at the time of our first confession at age seven about a perfect act of contrition. If one could be sorry for his sins, not because of a fear of hell or desire for heaven, but merely because one loved God, he could be forgiven his mortal sins (even though confession would be required later). This certainly tells the child that pre-conventional thinking is not sufficient or perfect, but it tells the child at an age when he cannot comprehend it. The child in order to make sense of it may begin to look at perfect contrition as an escape hatch. If one is bad, then the magic formula for saving oneself is the perfect act of contrition. Try as one might, a stage one person cannot get the fear of hell out of his mind, and he will probably want to make a perfect act of contrition in order to avoid going to hell. The point is that a concept of pure selfless love is quite incomprehensible to a child at stage one or two.

After stage two, one moves into the conventional level where there is group identification. It would follow that this is the time when a child identifies with the Church. He or she is in need of a community to define roles and duties.

The child at this stage will not be looking at religion or a religious group for what he can get out of it. The child wants to be a good boy or nice girl. Maintaining the expectations of the Church community, if one is visible, is valuable in its own right, regardless of the consequences. At this stage, stories of saints and heroes will have a profound effect on children. I remember being fascinated by St. Tarsisius, the boy who had to carry the Eucharist from one place to another. One day he met a group of boys who wanted to take it away from him. Tarsisius would not compromise on his duty. He was beaten to death. What was important was his fidelity to Christ and the Church. Whereas a child at stage one would not understand this, a child at stage three would be provided with a model. "This is the kind of boy the Church approves of." To be good, in the child's mind, is to perform the same sort of action.

Given the fact, however, that some adults are at stage three, we ought perhaps to say a few words about them. If the Church is important to people at stage three, that perspective would make unswerving attachment to the Church the desirable attitude. The good thing to do is that which the Church approves. Put yourself into the mind of such persons. They are not self-interested, except to the extent that they would like the approval of their Church. Chances are, if they are adults, they have lived on the basis of this group loyalty most of their·lives. The goal of their lives is approbation by the Church. Suppose they are now in their fifties or sixties. When they were young they learned that the good things to do, the actions the Church approved of, were daily Mass, bowed heads after communion, somberness and seriousness in church, not eating meat on Friday, fasting during Lent, etc., etc. Ten years ago, after a lifetime of doing the things the Church approved, they were told that the Church does not really care about those things. The fidelity to group practices that gave meaning to their lives was shattered, because although the Church still asked for fidelity, it did not specify in which practices this fidelity was to be exhibited. On the contrary, it said to many of these people: "The old way is not good enough." If Kohlberg's assessment is right, and if there *are* a number of adults reasoning at stage three, we get a new perspective on the kind of shock those people received when they were told that the old ways are not good enough. And when they asked about the new ways of being good (that is, an approved member of the Church), they were told that they must decide for themselves. The point is that, at their stage, the group must tell them what it expects. They were not told, and their road map for doing good was taken away and nothing was put in its place.

Kohlberg tells us that if individuals remain in a stage over too long a period of time, if they are not forced out of that stage, they may become *incapable* of moving to a higher level. If this is so, those who tend to be impatient with this basically selfless adherence to Church approval should be careful to recognize the real anguish of such stage three individuals, as well as the real possibility that they are locked into that stage.

In discussing the move to stage four, we saw that it was accepted because there was intellectual dissatisfaction with stage three. One of the factors which needed resolution was the conflicting goals or ends of various groups. In many cases there might be a conflict between what a family approves and what a Church approves. A classic example would be parents disapproving of a child's decision to devote himself to a religious life. Two resolutions are possible. One would be simply to give one's allegiance to one group or the other. The other more cognitive approach would be to look for an authority who could adjudicate such conflicts, an authority who is the custodian and interpreter of the laws. This resolution would be a stage four resolution.

It will be remembered that at stage four there is an orientation toward authority, fixed rules and the maintenance of the social order. Kohlberg does not specify the source and origin of this law, although it seems he has in mind the accepted social mores or a kind of natural law. But if one talks about religious content influencing our formal structures, then at stage four certain claims of the Church have a bearing on what we will accept as law and order. The Catholic Church has a long tradition of asserting that its hierarchical structure with the pope as its head, the teaching magisterium, has the responsibility of guiding its faithful in the laws of God. Thus, if at stage three, there is a conflict between fidelity to the family or the Church or between fidelity to the state and the Church, and if one is looking for a fixed order and authority, the Church makes a *special* claim of being that voice of authority. (It should be noted that in Nazi, Communist or despotic states, the state makes a similar claim. Hence, perhaps, the conflict between Church and state.) Thus, if our stage three person is looking for an arbiter between conflicting group claims and has a loyalty to the Church, his most natural move might be to accept unquestioningly the authority claimed for itself by the Church.

This move, I believe, is natural and has been made by a good many Church members. As stage four Church members they will be individuals exhibiting little or no egoism, but rather a selfless and passionate defense of the Church and its authorities as the defender of the correct order. It was not too long ago that a good deal of Christian formation appealed to unquestioning deference to the Church as the voice of God.

I remember interviewing a woman who was passionately devoted to the Church. When faced with the Heinz dilemma, she insisted that "stealing was wrong." For her that was an absolute, and no matter how one sympathized with Heinz and his wife, one could not justify the stealing. It was a violation of God's law. She was in a group with other people who insisted that life was more important than property. The woman's response was that God's law is the most important of all and that God would provide for Heinz and his wife after death.

Of course, one familiar with the Church's teachings would recognize that the moral theology of the Church can make provision for such a granting of priority to life over property. The Church's central concern, following Christ, has always been with the dignity of man who is a child of God. Consequently, I would suggest that the woman's view of the Church's morality was too limited. Nevertheless, it is a fact that a segment of the faithful have a rather rigid and fixed view of the laws of God and of his Church.

I believe that precisely at this point a good many Christians come to a fork in the road. The fork is created because of the theological belief. If God *is* omniscient, and if he is interested in the well-being of his people, and if he has given laws, they will be good laws and should be obeyed, for obedience to them will be rewarded. If that is one's belief, one is not going to be easily prodded into appreciating any questioning of this order as manifesting the highest level of moral reasoning. Questioning of the authority of the Church, which is the legitimate interpreter of God's laws and of the received law could be viewed as prideful arrogance.

This stage four reasoning raises difficulties that ought to be answered. If, indeed, there is an objective order of right and wrong, and if the Church is the legitimate interpreter of that order, then how can there be a higher stage of moral reasoning, for would not that reasoning be questioning the very law of God? Very often in lecturing, we have been asked whether or not Kohlberg's scheme is compatible with Christian or Catholic thought. What usually lies behind such a question is a concern about the proper relationship of man to God, especially God as the source of ultimate order and the promulgator of eternal law. The questioner may hold the belief that since God is the ultimate law-giver, there is a guarantee of an objective moral code. According to such a view, man's task is to find out what God wills, and to do it because he wills it and because it is the right thing to do. There seems to be little room for the autonomy of the fifth and sixth stages in such a view. Consequently, it might look as if stage four is the highest stage of development.

There is a great deal of plausibility in such a position, if one views God as a kind of biblical commander or as an ultimate orderer, which are models of God that are acceptable to many theologians. Still, it is important to remember that different commanders work in very different ways. A father is a commander of sorts and yet can put forth the rules of the house stringently, demanding strict observance, or he can put forth the rules and allow his children some leeway in their obedience to them. Need a commander expect *unquestioning* obedience? Further, doesn't a father often allow his children to venture out on their own so that they can discover for themselves how things are, even if this venturing may get them into trouble or cause them pain? Man learns by doing, and very often he learns most from his mistakes.

Consequently, even if one views God as a commander, this does not necessarily mean that he left nothing to our discretion, nothing to our own devices. But even if this is the case, is the model of the relationship of God to man, where God commands and man obeys unquestioningly, even an orthodox view? Vatican Council II stated explicitly:

Authentic freedom is an exceptional sign of the divine image within man. For God has willed that man be left "in the hand of his own counsel" (Sir. 15:4) so that he can seek his creator spontaneously and come freely to utter and blissful perfection through loyalty to him. Hence, man's dignity demands that he act according to a knowing and free choice. Such a choice is personally motivated and prompted from within. It does not result from blind internal impulse or from mere external pressure.[2]

This seems quite compatible with Kohlberg's ranking of stages, for what is necessary in the fifth, a post-conventional stage, is not a mere acceptance of laws which one has always obeyed, but critical (knowing) and free choice. Now, it is axiomatic that for a choice to occur one has to have at least two options available. Hence, a knowing and free choice must provide an opportunity to step out of a stage where there is pre-critical acceptance of a system of beliefs and values in order to compare that system with others.

As a matter of fact, does it not seem that Vatican Council II itself is encouraging a stage of reasoning higher than four by insisting that a man who freely chooses the Church and its laws has reached a higher stage of maturity than one who, having grown up into the practices of the Church, became conditioned to them, so that he is automatically in accord with them? A knowing and free choice is demanded by man's dignity.

Is not the post-conciliar Church, in effect, telling people that although it can give moral guidance, it cannot make up people's minds for them? Does it not insist that mature Christianity demands that people take responsibility for their own moral decisions? How then can the striving for autonomy be unorthodox?

Still, there is one consideration concerning Kohlberg's stages which may seem to clash with an "orthodox" view. Even the post-conciliar Church takes definitive stands on the morality and immorality of certain actions. It takes stands on abortion, pre-marital sex, etc. Within the Christian tradition, as we mentioned, the Church promulgates specific commands such as "Keep the Sabbath" or general imperatives for all men such as "Love your neighbor." Thus, we have these specific and general imperatives and it is generally viewed as wrong-doing if we disobey them.

It ought to be stressed that Kohlberg is not making value judgments about people at different stages, and furthermore he is not in the business of telling us what courses of action are right or wrong. He is a psychologist who is studying human growth in terms of moral reasoning, and while he does claim that one stage is higher than another, it is higher because it is cognitively more adequate as well as more in conformity with the freedom of decision that is demanded for a fully mature moral decision. Thus, while he may have personal feelings about whether something like abortion is right or wrong, as a psychologist he is only claiming that some reasons are more cognitively adequate and consequently exhibit more judgmental moral maturity.

But as Christians we are not merely viewing the world as psychologists. We are members of a community whose authorities do make moral judgments such as "Abortion is wrong" and maintain that these are correct judgments. How does one reconcile freedom of decision with that fact?

A study or resolution of this age old problem of the limits of freedom and the correlation of freedom and authority is not our purpose here. However, there *are* some distinctions and common sense considerations which, though they may not solve the problem completely, may indicate that Kohlberg's studies simply concentrate on one aspect of the situation. It has always been the practice in the Christian community to distinguish between an action and the motive for an action. Recall Christ's praising of the publican who prayed, not for social approval like the Pharisee, but to sincerely relate to God. Consider the man who gives alms out of concern for those poorer than himself, and the man who gives alms for the sake of praise.

There are always two ways of judging an action. We can judge the action itself as good or bad (we then talk about objective goodness or badness), or we can judge the reasons or intentions or motives of the person performing the action (we then talk about subjective goodness or badness). Obviously, given an objectively proper action, we prefer a higher motive or reason. That bespeaks moral maturity. Thus Kohlberg's scheme would be perfectly acceptable and compatible with Christian thought were we to concern ourselves with reasons for action, and indeed it provides us with a gauge as to the relative maturity of the reasons behind the action.

Let us assume a set of objectively valid moral maxims such as the ten commandments and let us assume that we want to educate ourselves and our children morally. It is not enough simply to teach someone that stealing is wrong. In teaching them that stealing is wrong, we want to concentrate on what is even more important than knowing that maxim. We want to concentrate on the reasons why it is wrong. Are we satisfied if they don't steal simply because it is forbidden? Don't we want them finally to come to see that stealing involves an injustice to others, and don't we know that to get them to see this means helping them mature in making moral judgments?

Most of us within the Christian community have been raised on the belief that pre-marital sexual intercourse is wrong. We have been more or less effective in teaching that rule. Still, how much attention have we paid to the individual's reasons for accepting such a rule. Are we satisfied with the maturity of one who simply avoids intercourse because of a fear of hell, or a fear of pregnancy and its unwanted consequences? Would we not hope for a development which would manifest more mature reasons? Or even more to the point, suppose someone engaged in pre-marital sexual intercourse, not out of overwhelming passion, but in the belief that it would be gratifying and beneficial to a distraught companion? Could we approve? Or again, to take a classic dilemma, suppose a woman during a war engaged in intercourse with a soldier who promised to save her child if she would. Do we approve? We have a choice to make. Given the option, would we want our children's strict adherence to the law, or would we prefer them to be capable of violating the law if they have good and honest reasons for so doing?

There is a tension here, and it shows two possible responses, concern for the letter of the law and concern for the spirit of the law. The Church at times is concerned with the development of the whole person and then it promulgates an ideal of freedom, but at other times it takes on the function of moral guardian and at those times it concerns itself with the promulgation of moral laws and encourages adherence to these laws.

This double faceted role has caused two different pedagogic techniques to be employed in the area of moral education. When acting as guardian of the faith the Church adopts the technique of teaching the correct moral precepts. The Church says: X is right and Y is wrong, etc. Very often then in this context one was judged morally mature when one simply behaved in accordance with those laws, and little or no attention was given to the reasons for the acqueiescence in these laws.

Simultaneously, however, the Church always concerned itself with developing virtues and mature dispositions. It always saw the highest state of man as a free embracing of the Will of God. Christ came to make us free, not automatons subject to the rules of a dictator. Any mature acceptance of Christ or the Father had to be a free spontaneous acceptance, not a conditioned reflex action.

What we learn from Kohlberg's studies and other psychological studies is that although a person might learn the list of do's and don'ts, there is little likelihood that he will internalize them. If the end of Christian moral education is mature moral development, it seems that the best course is to strive to raise the person's level of reasoning about moral issues. Why? Because here we know we can have some effect, whereas in the former method we know we have little effect.

We began this rather lengthy discussion by asking about the compatibility of Kohlberg's scheme with Christian orthodoxy. We hope that we have at least put some possible misapprehensions to rest. Still, I would like to draw one analogy. It seems to me that the Church today, when faced with educating its children to moral maturity, is very much in the same position as parents. As a parent, one wants to see one's children develop into self-sufficient individuals who are concerned for others and who think for themselves. Nevertheless, it is natural for a parent to want to protect his child from mistakes which will bring pain. Moreover, since a parent himself has practices and traditions which he loves and values, he cannot help but hope that his children will grow up to love them too. Realistically, however, one must realize that as children do grow into individuals, it is possible that they may reject what their parents value. Such a situation seems to be more the rule than the exception. A parent could perhaps forestall this cleavage between himself and his child by creating a relationship where the child is, and remains, excessively dependent on the parent. But such a relationship would merely serve to make the child an alterego of the parent rather than an individual unto himself. Such a symbiotic relationship ought to be avoided. The ideal situation, from the point of view of the parent, would seem to be a situation where the child, on his own, freely adopts and chooses the values his parent cherishes. This will allow a mature union of two adults in a community of beliefs and loves. Such a happy state of affairs may be quite rare, but it certainly seems worth the risk.

As I see it, the Church is in a position analogous to that of the parent. It does not need children who are excessively dependent on it. It needs and ought to encourage its children to become self-sufficient and to embrace it freely from that self-sufficiency. But, as in the case of the parents, such a program involves a risk. The child may not return. I suspect that this is precisely the kind of move the Church made in Vatican Council II. Recall pre-conciliar days. The "good" Catholic passionately believed in the system with its absolutes and fixed rules. Given the prohibitions on attending secular schools, on joining certain social organizations, and the index of forbidden books, the Catholic Church in the defensive post-Reformation stance effectively created a self-contained religious enclave. Yet, with the advent of the media explosion and the impetus toward getting into the mainstream of society, our Catholic and the Church itself became much like the man who left his protected but provincial valley. With the relaxing of restrictions against mixed marriages, the joining of organizations like the YMCA, the gradual disbanding of the index, and a host of other moves, the Church allowed its members to see how the other side thought and lived. As we have seen, this causes a person to see his group as ranging alongside other groups.

The Church in the aggiornamento period provoked the same sort of disequilibrium for its members as we saw provoked in those individuals who are passing into a stage four and one-half. The Church in seriously asking about its role looked upon its institutional forms as developing through time. Changing circumstances demanded changing responses, and a new understanding of the Church began to emerge. To those of us who had forgotten that the Church had a history, who forgot or who had never learned that the Church took different forms in different eras of history, the result was disconcerting. The view of other religious organizations moved from one where they were seen as largely in error to one where they were seen as participating in the guidance of the Holy Spirit. Our own Church was looked upon, so to speak, "from the outside" and was compared with other churches. The Church itself was questioning its own identity and values as manifested in many of its practices.

We saw when we reviewed stage four and one-half that such a looking at an institution from the outside can cause a skepticism, a relativism and an egoism based on an isolation from the group that one previously looked to for the source of infallible moral guidance. It seems not too wide of the mark to say that precisely this kind of skepticism, relativism and isolation from the Church occurred during the time of questioning that surrounded the days of Vatican II. But as with the case of parents and their children, so with the church: if the values it espouses and the practices it embraces speak to a person, he may return to such an organization. The difference will be that such will be a fully mature return, based on one's personal decision, and it will not be an allegiance that was simply a conditioned response.

Nevertheless, such a disequilibrium might cause some people to leave the Church. All of this, while it is painful to the Church, is a required risk if the Church desires its members to embrace it freely. Autonomy can be achieved, but at the expense of risk and a loss of the comfort of the certitude that accompanies stage four thinking.

We have suggested that the Church has created a state of disequilibrium for many of its people at a stage four level, and that this is painful. If we remember the characteristics of stage four and one-half, we will see the reasons for the pain. Skepticism replaces certitude, relativism replaces absolutism, and egocentricity replaces a previous group identity. The Church where one was nurtured, and which one thought a guaranteed instrument for peace, order and happiness, has fallen off of its pedestal. It is seen now not as a divine institution free from error, but as another human institution with all the frailties and limitations of human institutions. It would seem this transition through four and one-half is one time when there can be a severe crisis of faith (skepticism). Further, if one is cut off from intellectually accepting those beliefs and views which guided him through, binding him with others, he simultaneously faces a self-inflicted alienation from the community he had heretofore viewed as the source of the meaning of his life. The community and its people's goals and ends were his goals and ends. How can he be a part of them if he does not accept them? This state can only be one of anguished isolation and alienation. He must find goals for himself which will allow the re-establishing of his identity. But this search is a search alone and self-concerned—therefore a self-interested search.

Where stands the Christian educator in all of this? He cannot mouth "truths" to the skeptical person. He cannot ask him to turn back the clock and come home. These moves will be totally inefficacious. The Christian educator must stand by like the parent whose child has left home and can do no more than hope that the lost soul finds himself. Still, an understanding attitude can be helpful and can encourage another in his right and duty to freely find himself, even if it means suffering through the four and one-half person's rejections of all his former beliefs.

However, this view provides the four and one-half person with the unique opportunity to now freely choose the Church, because he can agree with its goals and ends and aspirations while recognizing its limitations. As we mentioned, there is a risk for the Church that the person may find the church wanting, and not return, but as in the prodigal son story, the best return is the return made freely, the embrace that rises from genuine affection, not from patterned reflex.

How many times have we heard anguished cries about children who have stopped going to church and have stopped using the sacraments? How many times have we tried to pressure these young to return to the right path? But how inefficacious that pressure is! Any return to be meaningful has to be a *free* return, not simply a return to please one's elders (that is stage three), but a return where the individual can see the value of the Church community.

There is a powerful film called "Workout" which depicts the inability of a father and son to come to agreement about the true meaning and values of life. The father seems to manifest a stage four level of thinking. He is strongly in favor of the laws and system, including the religious system, in which he was raised. He has come to his son's college to call him to account for getting involved in a protest. The father and son try to discuss the issues but do not communicate. The father seems oblivious to the son's doubts and questions. "When I went to college, they gave us the answers." The father is unable to appreciate why the son cannot accept his way of life and his values. One can read the boy's responses as stage four and one-half. But what is shown in the film, in an exceptionally good way, is the futility of the father's attempts. He threatens the boy with no money (a stage one motivation), offers the boy help if he will relent (stage two), appeals to his obligations to respect his father (stage three—role identification), and finally appeals to his son to accept what is right (stage four). But the son is beyond the attraction of these reasons, and in this case at least the child has become the father of the man.

Inevitably, the father gives up after a traumatic argument. Still, in the closing scene, after an uneasy truce has been achieved, there is a look of admiration for his son in the father's face—a look which says: I may not agree with you, I certainly do not understand you, but you are a self-sufficient man. That is something that makes me proud.

Still, let us suppose that this boy is at stage four and one-half. That means he is lonely and alone. Twice during the movie there is an affirmation of love. This, too, seems to reflect the way things are. A person at four and one-half, totally alone, needs to re-establish his ego. But, again, it is axiomatic that one cannot establish a self-identity independently of others. One's relationships with others make a person what he is. Now, at four and one-half, one can either hold himself off from others and live in egoistic isolation, where the other is over and against oneself, or one can attempt to positively relate to others, thereby giving up something of oneself by allowing the relation to the other to define oneself. This positive relating is the move toward love and a new socializing. Any positive relating to another is in effect the creating of a new society or a new move into an old society. If it proves at this point beneficial and fulfilling, loneliness is alleviated and a faith in the value of social living is restored. Such a faith is what brings about the destruction of the skepticism. Once it is established that we need others, stage five and six reasoning necessarily follow.

We have mentioned before two tracks that the Church seems to take in the issue of authority and freedom. On the one hand, it presents itself as the guardian of correct morals having the authority to interpret the law. On the other hand though, it is the defender and the instrument which liberates the individual. One can read the history of the Church as a struggle between these two tensions just as one can read a person at the post-conventional level as loving order yet subjecting it to rational scrutiny.

It will be remembered that the chief characteristic of principled thinking is the evaluation of the given system from an ideal perspective. One need only reflect on Christ's claim that he had not come to destroy the law but to fulfill it in order to find a model of principled thinking. Time and again the legalism of the Pharisees is challenged as destroying the spirit of the law. Time and again appeals are made to a higher order, the kingdom of God, which gave us an ideal by which to judge the real. Most important, however, were the appeals to the highest principles of all—justice and love, both based on the belief that we are all God's children, all beloved of God, and the insistence that even the highest authority should be the humblest servant.

If the highest level of moral reasoning is on a principled level, and if the highest principles are justice and love, and if justice and love are to be informed by a free choice, one is hard pressed to find a more consistent statement of such principles than in the New Testament.

IV
Practical Applications
of Moral Development Theory

Piaget and Kohlberg have established that growth in moral judgment is a developmental process. It is not a process of imprinting rules and virtues by modeling, lecturing, punishing and rewarding, but a process of cognitive restructuring. What then is the role of the parents and educators in the moral development of their children and adolescents, and, I might add, in their own moral development? Are there environmental conditions and/or adult actions that influence the process of development? Can school and church groups design programs that will facilitate moral development? In this section we will review the assumptions and qualities of a stage theory, draw from their implications the factors that influence development, and look at some of the means that research indicates are useful for facilitating moral development.

A developmental theory is posited on three assumptions:

1. Development involves basic transformations of structure, that is, the shape, pattern and organization of a response. We have seen this illustrated throughout Piaget and Kohlberg—for example, the transformation of structures necessary to go from heteronomy to autonomy. Individuals have a basic shape, pattern and organization to their moral reasoning. Development is a transformation of that basic structure to a structure that is more adequate.

2. Development is the result of a process of interactions between the structure and the organism and the environment. An in-

dividual is not passive in the process of development while some
biological process unfolds within. The importance of the environment is in the "continuity, organization and complexity of the
social and cognitive stimulation the child is exposed to."[1] Terry
Malloy, for example, in the film "On the Waterfront" is in an environment where decisions are made on the basis of personal well-
being. He is not challenged to reason otherwise until his environment is disrupted by an event that eventually leads him to reject
those standards that had previously satisfied him. The importance
of an environment capable of providing cognitive stimulation needs
to be stressed for those children who are deprived of intellectual
stimulation in their homes and neighborhoods, while the importance of social complexity should be taken into account for every
person, particularly those who are exposed to predominantly one
socio-economic, ethnic or religious group.

    3. The direction of development is toward greater equilibrium
in the organism-environment interaction. An individual who responds to moral questions on the basis of what the good husband
or good father should do will find the reasoning inadequate to
solve problems where society may conflict with family. This conflict leads to the development of more adequate structures for coping with the complexities of the environment-organism interaction.

    Several implications for moral education are apparent from
the assumptions of a developmental theory. Moral development,
because it involves basic transformations of cognitive structures, is
a slow, gradual process. Cognitive structures determine one's total
perspective, as we saw in moral realism. Moral development is not
changing one's point of view on a particular issue, but transform-
ing one's way of reasoning, expanding one's perspective to include
criteria for judging that were not considered previously. For instance, Kohlberg has found the majority of ten year olds on stages
one and two until about age thirteen, when stage three and four
reasoning tends to increase. Roughly then, for the first sixteen to
twenty years of life one is working through four stages of development.

    The assumptions of a stage theory state clearly that develop-
ment is not automatic. The quality of the social environment has a
significant influence on the rate of development and the level of

development one achieves. This is clearer, I think, when we consider point three, that the motivating principle of development is equilibrium, that is, the resolution of cognitive conflict. The organism seeks to construct adequate cognitive structures to cope with its social environment. Hence, an intellectually impoverished environment does not motivate development, because only minimal structures are needed for coping. If, for example, a principle like "Don't be a stoolie and you won't get hurt" resolves most of the problems in a neighborhood, there is no conflict of values to create a disturbance of equilibrium between the individual and his society. If, however, an individual lives in a community differentiated in its values and norms, confrontation of various influences is inevitable. This kind of social environment will create the disequilibrium that is essential for moral development.

It will be helpful now to look again at the qualities of a moral development stage theory for factors that can influence moral education. Under this theory, a successful educational approach to moral development will not emphasize the traditional strategies of modeling, lecturing, rewarding and punishing; rather the approach will be based on the educational implications of the following qualities of stage theory:

1. Development is step by step, that is, the stages are invariant. I think this is understandable if one reflects on the structural transformation that is involved in moving from one stage to another. There are conservative factors that moderate development so that it is never a radical departure from all familiar elements. Hence, a stage two person, an egoist, does not leap into stage four, societal considerations. He gradually moves from egoism to stage three, group considerations, such as family or peers, and then to stage four, the larger society. This is an important fact for designing educational programs suitable to the stage of development and for setting expectations that are realistic.

2. Development can terminate at any stage. Kohlberg has found in his prison studies that many inmates reason from stage two structures. The majority of adults are probably stage four, but some develop to stages five and six. An environment lacking social and cognitive stimulation such as Terry Malloy's in "On the Waterfront" would provide little incentive for development and con-

tribute toward the premature termination of many of its members at stages one and two. The educator's role is to create conditions that stimulate maximum development for each individual, primarily by stimulating higher levels of reasoning.

3. An individual's reasoning is predominantly one stage, with occasional reasoning one stage above or one stage below. This points out the importance of obtaining a broad sampling of an individual's responses before a judgment is made about the stage of moral development.

4. An individual can be attracted to reasoning one stage higher than his predominant stage. He is not attracted to reasoning a stage below. Thus, a stage two egoist will not be attracted to reasoning based on fear of punishment, but could be stimulated to considerations of family or classmates or Scout troop loyalty. This quality of stage theory accounts in part for the effectiveness of moral discussion groups where participants at various stages of development discuss dilemmas together.

5. Development is not governed by age. Rate of development varies. Some young people achieve higher stages than older adults. As will be pointed out later, there are certain ranges of ages that are good predictors of stages between the ages of twelve and twenty, but the important point is that rate will vary even within the same family.

6. Cognitive development is necessary, but not a sufficient condition for moral development. Abstract reasoning ability is essential to entertain alternatives in moral reasoning and to order priorities in values. One reason why children under twelve cannot be expected to attain higher stages of moral development is because those stages require more sophisticated cognitive abilities than young children possess, primarily the ability to reason abstractly.

7. Empathy is also necessary, but not a sufficient condition for moral development. It is through empathy that one develops an understanding of what a community is and begins to judge actions as right or wrong on the basis of mutual respect. This is a quality of stage theory that both parents and educators can focus on with profit. Some strategies for developing empathy will be mentioned later in this chapter.

In summary, then, the principles of development in moral judgment are stated in the assumptions and qualities of a developmental theory. The aim of education in moral judgment is to insure optimal development for each individual. The factors that influence moral development are the social environment, cognitive development, empathy and cognitive conflict. The importance of moral education is apparent from the research indicating that children who fail to develop for a number of years are likely to become locked in at their stage.[2]

If the goal of moral education is optimal development for each individual and if the factors influencing development are the social environment—primarily the cognitive stimulation of the social environment—cognitive development, and empathy, then education programs should be geared to the level of the individual and should focus on modifying those environmental and personal factors that influence development. Methodology should be derived from the principles of development stated in the assumptions and qualities of a stage theory. We will discuss techniques and procedures for two aspects of moral education: creating cognitive stimulation and developing empathy.

To create cognitive stimulation in a moral education program is to upset the equilibrium of the individual by setting up a situation where he experiences sufficient conflict in resolving a problem to realize that his reasoning structures are too limited to include the new perspectives the conflict is intended to present. This can be done effectively in moral education groups which will be discussed later in the chapter. As indicated in the qualities of stage theory, cognitive conflict is only experienced when the considerations being introduced emanate from one stage above the individual's usual stage of reasoning about moral conflicts. Neither one stage below nor two stages above will create conflict. The first step, then, in creating cognitive stimulation is to determine the individual's predominant mode of moral reasoning.

The skill of assessing stages of moral reasoning is only acquired by a thorough understanding of the stage descriptions, including an ability to apply those descriptions to particular responses and to analyze the elements of each stage and the relationships among the stages. A person with this type of understanding, together with experience in analyzing responses, can de-termine with some validity and reliability the actual stage of an-other individual. The Ontario Institute for Studies in Education has published an excellent guide (see Bibliography) intended to provide teachers with a method to develop the skill for measuring the degree of moral development reached by their students. Teach-ers can also follow the rough age-stage guide that Kohlberg has drawn up—that is, that most ten to fourteen year olds are on stages one and two, while fourteen to sixteen year olds are on stages three and four.

To assess the development of the younger children, ages six to nine, is basically to determine whether they are heteronomous or autonomous on a particular issue, and Piaget's dilemmas provide situations that are comprehensible and relevant for this purpose, though some of the stories need to be updated. The emphasis in the questioning about each story should be to find out why the child thinks a particular action is right or wrong, or comparatively worse than another action.

Assessing the stage of moral reasoning, then, is the first step to an education program that is directed toward stimulating cogni-tive conflict. The second step is to match the individual's stage of reasoning by confronting him with reasoning one stage higher. Thus, if a child's predominant stage is Kohlberg's two, where deci-sions are made on the basis of satisfying one's needs, the educa-tor's role is to clarify for the child his present mode of reasoning and then insert level three reasoning into the discussion. For exam-ple, if one were discussing the Joe dilemma, a stage two might say, "Well, if he wants to give it to the father, he should give it to him; if he doesn't want to give it to him, he doesn't have to!" To clarify for the child his own reasoning, one might ask "Why might Joe not give his father the money?" or "What things should Joe think about in this problem?" To insert level three reasoning, one could simply raise other questions that ought to be considered, ones that focus on the next stage, such as "Do you think the father is setting a good example?" or "What kinds of things does a father usually do for his son?" The type of questions that would not be educative at this stage—and, according to the theory, could not even be comprehended—would be ones that appeal to stage four, with concerns about the father's authority or the son's obligation to respect and obey the father.

In matching, one is concerned not only to present the higher level of reasoning, but also to create disequilibrium about the application of the current level of thought.

Kohlberg has found that one successful means of creating cognitive stimulation is through moral education groups where the discussion is aimed at exposing students to higher levels of thought and at creating cognitive conflict in their current level of thought. The moral discussion groups designed by Blatt and Kohlberg consisted of ten to twelve students at different stages of moral development. These students engaged in twice-weekly discussions of moral dilemmas, some hypothetical, some personal, some real-social. Controversy between the two lowest stages, two and three, was first encouraged, with the leader clarifying and to some extent supporting the higher stage. When there seemed to be some movement of the lower stage students, controversy was focused on the next two stages. Kohlberg's research data indicate that students who participated in these discussion groups showed upward change in moral development.[3]

It is important to note that the moral educator is not evaluating the rightness or wrongness of another's reasoning stage, nor imposing adult "right" answers to the dilemmas. No amount of lecturing, punishing, or rewarding will modify the basic reasoning structure. This is not easy for parents and other educators who see their role to be one of providing answers to accept. Most adults can seriously question their own level of moral development when findings indicate that the majority of adults are stage four and that only a minority move to stage five, and fewer to stage six. If most adults are stage four, they can approach moral discussion groups in a role as leaders or participants with as many questions about the dilemmas as the other participants have. Theirs can be an honest search for the inadequacies of their own reasoning, for insight into those principles that are influencing their decisions and the principles that are not influencing their decisions. And these insights may be revealed by adolescents in the group, since age does not govern stages of moral reasoning.

A very important aspect of moral development to both Piaget

and Kohlberg is the development of empathy. I think it is clear that though moral judgment is primarily a function of rational operations, affectional factors like empathy expand an individual's perspective and allow him to take other viewpoints. Some ways of developing powers of empathy have been mentioned in the Piaget sections. We will recall and expand on them now in a list of suggested broad areas:

1. Quietly sitting with a child to discuss with him the effects on the family or class of some irresponsible action of his.

2. Helping a child work through a decision by provoking consideration of the feelings of others who will be affected by the decision—for example, whether to cancel an earlier commitment to play with a friend when a more interesting invitation is issued from another friend.

3. Adults sharing with children their feelings about encounters or events that affect them.

4. Helping children clarify their feelings about encounters or events that affect them.

5. Acknowledging and discussing with the children those times when their actions or presence was a source of joy, pleasure, courage or comfort.

Basically we want to help children develop a sense of community in the family, the classroom and all of the groups to which they belong. Later this understanding of community will expand to include the larger community of mankind, but the quality of concern at that time is dependent on the earlier sensitivity to smaller communities.

Empathy and mutual respect should be the focus of moral education programs for young children, since it is the ability to understand from another's perspective that enables them to participate more fully in the family, school and peer communities. It is this function, the developing of empathy by stimulating the child to put himself in another's position, that Kohlberg has found to be the most important contribution of the family in moral development.[4]

In other settings more structured than the family, one means of developing empathy is role-playing. This is effective with children, adolescents, and adults. A child assigned the role of school counselor is forced to consider other perspectives as he counsels a child role-playing a difficult sibling relationship, or teacher-pupil tension. Even those observing the role-playing have the opportunity to consider a problem from different perspectives.

Any dilemma, hypothetical or real, can be role-played to advantage, either with the participants taking roles spontaneously and acting in the manner they think the individual would act, or with each participant being assigned a role with a particular moral stage which is to influence all of his dialogue. So, for example, let Heinz and the druggist and the wife interact spontaneously to see one another's perspective. Or assign Heinz a stage three orientation, the druggist a stage four and the wife a stage four, and let the dialogue proceed spontaneously, each one focusing on the reasons for doing what he or she is doing, using reasons consonant with the stage assigned. This provides opportunities for confronting different levels of reasoning as well as for gaining another's perspective.

In December 1973, newspapers reported the death of an elderly couple in Schenectady, New York. Frank and Catherine Baker, 92 and 91 respectively, were found on Christmas Eve frozen to death after their electricity which was needed to run the furnace had been shut off because they had not paid their bill. An incident like this presents a real moral dilemma at many levels of decision-making, and it can be used for role-playing by defining the roles and job descriptions, and then having those company personnel meet to discuss the problems, with the focus on each person deciding what the company should do and why. This forces the group to look at the problem from a number of different perspectives.

It is important to mention at this point that the dilemmas for role-playing or for discussion should be genuine moral conflicts, that is, problems involving justice and human welfare in such situations as life, property rights, law, conscience, truth, and authority. Questions of good manners, courtesy and classroom order generally do not have the substance to constitute a moral conflict. We have included in the Appendix Piaget's and Kohlberg's dilemmas.

In addition to developing empathy, role-playing designated stages makes a useful means of teaching the stages to adults, and presumably could be used with adolescents for the same purpose. Several individuals in a group could be asked to discuss a dilemma while the rest of the group observes. Each discussant could be assigned a specific stage to assume for reasoning about the dilemma. Thus, if the power company dilemma were used as the content of discussion and the question were asked "What would you do if you were the lineman?" each discussant would respond and support his decision with reasons that were consistent with the stage he had been assigned. Thus a person role-playing stage two might respond, "Yes, I'd turn off the line; if I didn't, I'd lose my job." At the conclusion of the dilemma discussion the group of observers tries to determine the role-played stage of each of the actors and discusses further the characteristics of the stages. This type of activity raises questions that clarify the distinctions between the stages and leads the participants to a firmer understanding of the diversity of reasons that emanate from the cognitive structure of each stage.

A very good means of achieving all three educational goals—that is, creating cognitive stimulation, developing empathy, and teaching a better understanding of the stages—is the use of films. Any feature or documentary that provides enough dialogue for the viewer to perceive the reasons for the actions of the characters is suitable.

"On the Waterfront" is one such film. Terry, Edy and the priest engage in dialogue that reveals their motivation for action. One of Terry's earliest statements "Don't be a stoolie and you won't get hurt" provides the clue to the pain-pleasure orientation that forms Terry's reasoning in the early part of the film. His association with Edy, the sister of the boy whom Terry was instrumental in slaying, provokes him to consider things from her perspective as well as his own. As a caring relationship develops, Terry, exasperated by Edy's persistent queries, explains his reluctance to give her any information on her brother's death by saying, "I'm only trying to prevent you from getting hurt; what more do you want?" Terry is speaking now from an orientation broader than his own pain and pleasure. This development continues amid violent circumstances to a point where Terry sees beyond himself, beyond his relationship with Edy, to considerations of justice for all the union workers, while Edy serves as a catalyst affecting Terry, the priest and her own father.

Documentary films like "Sixteen in Webster Groves" or "A

Time for Burning" which portray discussions of values and reasons for action are valuable for analysis. "Sixteen in Webster Groves" counterpoints parents and teenagers of an upper middle class St. Louis suburb in a discussion of values and goals, while "A Time for Burning" focuses on a parish discussing action to be taken in the area of race relations. Both films have ample material for analysis of stages. "Workout," mentioned earlier, is an excellent film for analyzing stages four and four and one-half.

The principles of moral development theory can be useful guides to the type of correction to be given for deviant behavior. Two facts should be kept in mind,

1. The child or adolescent cannot comprehend reasons for not behaving as he did that are more than one stage above his development. Therefore the parent or teacher should not impose on the child adult reasons for not behaving in the deviant manner, but rather solicit from the child or adolescent the reasons why he thought the action was right. Appeal, then, to reasons that might yield a different conclusion, but that are from the same stage as his reasoning and from one stage above.

2. A child or adolescent will reject reasons for not behaving as he did that are below his level of development. A correction thus delivered may provide no motivation for reform. Therefore the parent or teacher generally should not resort to threats of punishment or hopes of reward as an appeal to change reasoning about behavior. Once again it is important to discern the child's reasons for behaving as he did, and then to avoid suggesting reasons that are below his. For example, if a stage two child is being reprimanded by his parents for shoplifting, to tell him it's wrong because he has broken the law, and that he should respect the shopkeeper's right to property, is to appeal to him with stage four reasoning to which he is not attracted because he cannot fully comprehend it. Conversely, to say it is wrong because he can get arrested and punished is to appeal to him from stage one, which is inadequate for him.

The difficulties children have in comprehending a stage above their own was revealed in studies of children's comprehension of the golden rule, "Do unto others as you would have them do unto you."[5] All the children, ages ten to sixteen, knew the rule and were able to repeat it. Their interpretation of it, however, emanated directly from their moral development stage. Thus, to the stage two children, if someone hits you, the way you apply the golden rule is to hit him back. For them reciprocity is blow for blow. Stage two children also interpreted the golden rule to mean: If you're nice to people, they'll be nice back to you.[6]

In summary then, in light of the theories of Piaget and Kohlberg, the role of the moral educator is to help the child, adolescent or adult to think about the reasoning he uses to resolve genuine moral conflicts, to see inadequacies in his reasoning, and to lead him to more adequate structures. To do this it is necessary to know the level of thought, to match that level of thought by communicating one level above, to focus on reasoning, and to help the person experience the cognitive conflict that will make him aware of the greater adequacy of the next stage.

Obviously this approach to moral education is not going to bring about any quick solutions to the problems of moral behavior that confront parents and social institutions. However, if you recall the Piaget discussion on rules, when rules were mutually derived, agreed upon, and understood, there was greater fidelity in the practice of them. This can be attributed to the higher level of motivation. Kohlberg has found a similar relationship between higher levels of moral development and moral behavior. In experimental studies of cheating behavior[7] the majority of lower stage subjects cheated a great deal or a moderate amount, while only a tenth of the subjects at higher stages did any cheating at all.[7] In another study (Freundlich and Kohlberg) eighty-three percent of delinquent adolescents were found to be pre-conventional, stages one or two.[8] Kohlberg points out that while there are a great many factors contributing to delinquency, it would appear that levels of moral development above stages one and two at least serve as a deterrent to delinquent behavior.

A knowledge of the principles of developmental theories or moral judgment does not simplify the task of educating for moral development. The questions of content selection, organization, motivational strategies, and providing for individual differences still have to be answered, and patience, tolerance and understanding still are essential. This knowledge does, however, provide the basis for a rational approach to moral development, and, as we have shown, the effects of expanding a person's perspective and reasoning structures are lasting. It is the focus on reasoning and the wide-range effects of any one person's development that we hope will inspire parents and educators to respond to the challenge of insuring optimal development for as many children and adolescents as possible.

Practical Rules for Parents

1. Do not equate rule observance with moral development.
2. Be attentive to and actively solicit children's reasons for their moral judgments.
3. Do not evaluate reasons as good or bad, nor decisions as right or wrong.
4. Make distinctions in your concern between rules for good manners and good household order and issues of moral substance concerning justice and human relations.
5. Provide opportunities for children to participate in deciding rules for common living in the family.
6. Do not try to stimulate the child's moral reasoning when you are in the heat of anger and aggravation over his behavior.
7. Choose punishments that relate to the specific offenses and that emphasize the effect of behavior on the community.
8. Try not to react with more aggravation or disgust to children's carelessness than you would to the same action committed by an adult.
9. Temper your reaction to the young child's distasteful epithets and imaginative fibs.
10. Respect the child's right to an apology when you have been unjust in condemnation or judgment.
11. Be patient with the middle age child's delicate sense of justice when he refuses to perform even an inconsequential act like closing the door because he judges the command unfair, that is, he was not the last one in. If possible do not resort to an authoritarian role, but convey to him the understanding that you are asking him for a favor. (N.B. He may still refuse!)

12. Periodically discuss with the children what they consider to be fair and unfair in the family relationships and procedures.

13. Let middle age and older children assume responsibility for establishing procedures for dividing up the household chores and responsibilities.

14. Discuss contemporary issues that involve moral decisions, urging each child to articulate his position and reasons, but be careful not to evaluate any responses or decisions as right or wrong, or as better or best.

15. Focus on reasons for judgment, not on the child's behavior.

16. Try to be realistic in your expectations, remembering that it is approximately twenty years before the young adult judges from the perspective of the general social order.

17. Set up structures for living and articulate your expectations for conduct, but remember that you cannot imprint your values on your progeny. In order to construct their own system of values they have to rethink and order those which you projected.

Practical Rules for Teachers

1. Focus on establishing the classroom as a community where the participants will live and learn together in an atmosphere of respect and security.

2. Provide opportunities for the children to have a voice in establishing the rules of the classroom.

3. Choose punishments that relate to the offense, stressing with the child, where possible, the effect of his action on the group.

4. Make distinctions between criticism of academic work and criticism of behavior, and between rules for the good order of the school and rules affecting justice and human relations.

5. Provide opportunities for peer group work.

6. In stories and discussions of everyday experience, help the children to consider the feelings of other real or fictional persons.

7. Role-play experiences from daily life, events that lead to disappointments, tensions, fights, joys, in order to provide opportunities for the pupils to see the event from perspectives other than their own.

8. Discuss with the class what they consider fair and unfair classroom procedures and relationships.

9. Frequently take time to listen to each student's responses to questions of moral judgment, and stimulate discussions that will provoke higher stage reasoning, using literature, film and life experiences.

10. Avoid making judgments about moral development on the basis of behavior. People from six different stages might perform the same action, but for different reasons.

Appendix I
Piaget's Stories
for Moral Judgment [1]

Stories of Carelessness

I. A. A little boy named John is in his room. He is called to dinner. He goes into the dining room. But behind the door there is a chair, and on the chair there is a tray with fifteen cups on it. John couldn't have known that all this was behind the door. He goes in, the door knocks against the tray, bang go the fifteen cups and they all get broken.

B. Once there was a little boy whose name was Henry. One day when his mother was out he tried to get some jam out of the cupboard. He climbed up onto a chair but he couldn't reach it. However, while he was trying to get it he knocked over a cup. The cup fell down and broke.

II. A. There was a little boy named Julian. His father had gone out and Julian thought it would be fun to play with his father's inkwell. First he played with the pen, and then he made a little blot on the tablecloth.

B. A little boy named Augustus once noticed that his father's inkwell was empty. One day, when his father was away, he decided to fill the inkwell in order to help his father, so that he would find it full when he came home. But while he was opening the ink bottle, he made a big blot on the tablecloth.

III. A. A little girl named Marie wanted to give her mother a nice surprise and cut out a piece of sewing for her. But she didn't know how to use the scissors properly and cut a big hole in her dress.

B. A little girl named Margaret took her mother's scissors one day when her mother was out. She played with them for a while. Then, because she didn't know how to use them properly, she made a little hole in her dress.

When we have analyzed the answers obtained by means of these pairs of stories, we shall study two problems relating to stealing. Since our aim for the moment is to find out whether the child pays more attention to motive or to material results, we have presented acts of stealing with those that are well-intentioned.

Stories of Stealing

IV. A. Alfred meets a friend who is very poor. This friend tells him that he has had no dinner that day because there was nothing to eat in his home. Then Alfred goes into a baker's shop, and since he has no money, he waits until the baker's back is turned and steals a roll. Then he runs out and gives the roll to his friend.

B. Henriette goes into a shop. She sees a pretty piece of ribbon on a table and thinks to herself that it would look very nice on her dress. So, while the saleslady's back is turned, she steals the ribbon and runs away at once.

V. A. Albertine had a little friend who kept a bird in a cage. Albertine thought the bird was very unhappy, and she was always asking her friend to let him out, but the friend wouldn't. So one day when her friend wasn't there, Albertine stole the bird. She let it fly away and hid the cage in the attic so that the bird would never be shut up in it again.

B. Juliet stole some candy from her mother one day when her mother was not there. She hid and ate them.

Stories of Lying

I. A. A little boy goes for a walk in the street and meets a big dog who frightens him very much. He goes home and tells his mother he has seen a dog that was as big as a cow.

B. A child comes home from school and tells his mother that the teacher has given him good marks, but it is not true; the teacher has given him no marks at all, either good or bad. His mother is very pleased and rewards him.

II. A. A boy was playing in his room. His mother called and asked him to deliver a message for her. He didn't feel like going out, so he told his mother that his feet were hurting. But it wasn't true. His feet weren't hurting him in the least.

B. A boy wanted very much to go for a ride in a car, but no one ever asked him. One day he saw a man driving a beautiful car. When he got home he told his parents that the gentleman in the car had stopped and had taken him for a little drive. But it was not true; he had made it all up.

III. A. A boy couldn't draw very well, but he would have liked very much to be able to draw. One day he was looking at a beautiful drawing that another boy had done, and he said: "I made that drawing."

B. A boy was playing with the scissors one day when his mother was out and he lost them. When his mother came in he said that he hadn't seen them and hadn't touched them.

IV. A. A child who didn't know the names of streets very well was not quite sure where Main Street was. One day a gentleman stopped him in the street and asked him where Main Street was. So the boy answered, "I think it is that way." But it was not. The gentleman completely lost his way and could not find the house he was looking for.

B. A boy knew the names of streets quite well. One day a gentleman asked him where Main Street was. But the boy wanted to play a trick on him, and he said: "It's there." He showed him the wrong street, but the gentleman didn't get lost and managed to find his way again.

Stories of Punishment

I. A mother tells her three boys that they must not play with the scissors while she is out. But as soon as she is gone, the first one says, "Let's play with the scissors." Then the second boy goes to get some newspapers to cut out. The third one says, "No! Mother said we shouldn't. I won't touch the scissors." When the mother comes home, she sees all the bits of cut-up newspaper on the floor. She knows that someone has been touching her scissors, and she punishes all three boys. Was that fair?

II. After coming out of school, some boys started throwing snowballs at each other. One of the boys accidentally broke a window of a house with a snowball. The owner comes out and asked who did it. Since no one answered, he complained to the principal. The next day the principal asked the class who broke the window. But again, no one spoke. The boy who had done it said that it wasn't he, and the others wouldn't tell on him. What should the master do? (If the child does not answer or misses the point, you can add details to make things clearer.) Ought he to punish no one, or the whole class?

III. Some boys were throwing snowballs against a wall. They were allowed to do this, but on condition that they did not throw them too high, because above the wall there was a window, and the windowpanes might get broken. The boys had a wonderful time— all except one who was rather clumsy and who was not very good at throwing snowballs. When no one was looking, he picked up a rock and put it in the middle of a snowball. Then he threw it, and it went so high that it struck the window, broke the windowpane, and fell into the room. When the father came home he saw what had happened. He even found the rock with some melted snow on the floor. He was angry and asked who had done this. But the boy who had done it said it wasn't he, and so did the others. They did not know that he had put a rock in his snowball. What should the father do—punish everyone, or no one?

IV. During a school outing, the teacher allowed the children to play in a barn, on condition that they put everything back where they found it before going away. Some of them took rakes, others took spades, and they all went off in different directions. One of the boys took a wheelbarrow and played by himself, until he accidentally broke it. Then he came back when no one was looking and hid the wheelbarrow in the barn. In the evening when the teacher looked to see if everything was tidy, he found the broken wheelbarrow and asked who had done it. But the boy who had done it said nothing, and the others didn't know who it was. What should have been done? (Should the whole class be punished or no one?)

V. There was a school with only two classes—a class of older children and a class of younger ones. One day, when they had finished their schoolwork, the younger children asked the older ones to lend them one of their beautiful animal books. The older ones did so, telling them to take good care of it. Two of the younger children tried to turn to different pages at the same time. They quarreled, and some of the pages of the book got torn. When the older ones saw that the book was torn, they declared that they would never lend it to the younger children again. Were they right or not?

VI. A mother gave her three little boys a lovely box of colored crayons and told them to be very careful not to drop them so that they wouldn't get broken. But one of them who drew badly saw that his brothers were making better drawings than he was, and out of spite he threw all the crayons on the floor. When the mother saw this, she took the crayons away and never gave them back to the children again. Was she right to do this or not?

Stories of Immanent Justice

I. Once there were two children who were stealing apples in an orchard. Suddenly a policeman came along and the two children ran away. One of them was caught. The other one, going home by a roundabout way, crossed a rotting bridge over a river and fell into the water. Now what do you think? If he had not stolen the apples and still had crossed the river on that rotten bridge, would he also have fallen into the water?

II. In a class of very little children the teacher had forbidden them to sharpen their pencils themselves. Once, when the teacher had her back turned, a little boy took the knife and was going to sharpen his pencil, but he cut his finger. If the teacher had allowed him to sharpen his pencil, would he have cut himself just the same?

III. There was a little boy who disobeyed his mother. He took the scissors one day when he had been told not to. But he put them back in their place before his mother came home, and she never noticed anything. The next day he went for a walk and crossed a stream on a little bridge. It gave way, and he fell in the water with a splash. Why did he fall into the water? (And if he had not disobeyed, would he still have fallen in?)

Stories of Justice and Authority

I. Once there was a camp for Boy Scouts (or Girl Scouts). Each one had to do his bit to help with the work and leave things tidy. One had to do the shopping, another brought in wood or swept the floor. One day there was no bread and the one who did the shopping had already gone. So the Scoutmaster asked one of the Scouts who had already done his job to go and fetch the bread. What did he do?

II. One Thursday afternoon, a mother asked her little girl and boy to help her around the house because she was tired. The girl was to dry the plates and the boy was to fetch some wood. But the little boy (or girl) went out and played in the street, so the mother asked the other one to do all the work. What did he (she) say?

III. Once there was a family with three brothers. The two younger brothers were twins. They all used to polish their shoes every morning. One day the oldest brother was ill, so the mother asked one of the others to polish the brother's shoes as well as his own. What do you think of that?

IV. A father had two boys. One of them always grumbled when he was sent on messages. The other one didn't like being sent either, but he always went without saying a word. So the father used to send the boy who didn't grumble more often than the other one. What do you think of that?

Appendix II
Kohlberg's Moral
Judgment Situations[1]

I. Joe is a fourteen year old boy who wanted to go to camp very much. His father promised him he could go if he saved up the money for it himself. So Joe worked hard at his paper route and saved up the $40 it cost to go to camp and a little more besides. But just before camp was going to start, his father changed his mind. Some of his friends decided to go on a special fishing trip, and Joe's father was short of the money it would cost. So he told Joe to give him the money he had saved from the paper route. Joe didn't want to give up going to camp, so he thought of refusing to give his father the money.—Should Joe refuse to give his father the money or should he give it to him? Why?

I. A. Joe lied and said he only made $10 and went to camp with the other $40 he made. Joe had an older brother named Bob. Before Joe went to camp, he told Bob about the money and about lying to their father.—Should Bob tell their father? Why?

II. In Europe, a woman was near death from a special kind of cancer. There was one drug that the doctors thought might save her. It was a form of radium that a druggist in the same town had recently discovered. The drug was expensive to make, but the druggist was charging ten times what the drug cost him to make. He paid $200 for the radium and charged $2,000 for a small dose of the drug. The sick woman's husband, Heinz, went to everyone he knew to borrow the money, but he could only get together about $1,000, which is half of what it cost. He told the druggist that his wife was dying and asked him to sell it cheaper or let him pay later. The druggist said, "No, I discovered the drug and I'm going to make money from it." So Heinz got desperate and broke into the man's store to steal the drug for his wife.—Should the husband have done that? Why?

II. A. The doctor finally got some of the radium drug for Heinz' wife, but it didn't work, and there was no other treatment known to medicine which could save her. The doctor knew that she had only about six months to live. She was in terrible pain, but she was so weak that a good dose of a painkiller like ether or morphine would make her die sooner. She was delirious and almost crazy with pain, and in her calm periods she would ask the doctor to give her enough ether to kill her. She said she couldn't stand the pain and she was going to die in a few months anyway.—Should the doctor do what she asks and make her die to put her out of her terrible pain? Why?

II. B. While all this was happening, Heinz was in jail for breaking in and trying to steal the medicine. He had been sentenced for ten years. But after a couple of years he escaped from the prison and went to live in another part of the country under a new name. He saved money and slowly built up a big factory. He gave his workers the highest wages and used most of his profits to build a hospital for work in curing cancer. Twenty years had passed when a tailor recognized the factory owner as being Heinz the escaped convict whom the police had been looking for back in his home town.—Should the tailor report Heinz to the police? Why?

III. In Korea, a company of Marines was greatly outnumbered and was retreating before the enemy. The company had crossed a bridge over a river, but the enemy were still mostly on the other side. If someone went back to the bridge and blew it up as the enemy soldiers were coming over it, it would weaken the enemy. With the head start the rest of the men in the company would have, they could probably then escape. But the man who stayed back to blow up the bridge would probably not be able to escape alive; there would be about a 4 to 1 chance that he would be killed. The captain of the company has to decide who should go back and do the job. The captain himself is the man who knows best how to lead the retreat. He asks for volunteers, but no one will volunteer.—Should the captain order a man to stay behind, or stay behind himself, or leave nobody behind? Why?

III. A. The captain finally decided to order one of the men to stay behind. One of the men he thought of had a lot of strength and courage but he was a bad troublemaker. He was always stealing things from the other men, beating them up and refusing to do his work. The second man he thought of had gotten a bad disease in Korea and was likely to die in a short time anyway, though he was strong enough to do the job.—If the captain was going to send one of the two men, should he send the troublemaker or the sick man? Why?

IV. Two young men were in trouble. They were secretly leaving town in a hurry and needed money. Karl, the older one, broke into a store and stole $500. Bob, the younger one, went to a man who was known to help people in town. Bob told the man that he was very sick and needed $500 to pay for his operation. He really wasn't sick at all, and he had no intention of paying the money back. Although the man didn't know Bob very well, he loaned him the money. So Karl and Bob skipped town, each with $500.— Which would be worse, stealing like Karl or cheating like Bob? Why? Suppose Bob had gotten the loan from a bank with no intention of paying it back. Is borrowing from the bank or the old man worse? Why? What do you think is the worst thing about cheating the old man? Why shouldn't someone steal from a store? What is the value or importance of property rights? Which would be worse in terms of society's welfare—cheating like Bob or stealing like Karl? Why?

V. During the war in Europe, a city was often heavily bombed. All the men in the city were assigned to different fire-fighting and rescue stations all over the city. A man named Diesing was in charge of one fire engine station near where he worked. One day after an especially heavy bombing, Diesing left the shelter to go to his station. But on the way, he decided that he had to see whether his family was safe. His home was quite far away, but he went there first.—Was it right or wrong for him to leave the station to protect his family?

Bibliography

Beck, Clive, *Moral Education in the Schools.* Toronto: Toronto Institute For Students in Education, 1971. Practical ideas on teaching of moral education from kindergarten through senior high school.

Beck, C. M., B. S. Crittenden and E. V. Sullivan (eds.), *Moral Education, Interdisciplinary Approaches.* New York: Newman Press, 1971.

Blatt, M. Kohlberg, L. "The Effects of Classroom Moral Discussion Upon Children's Level of Moral Judgment." Research report found in *Collected Papers on Moral Development and Moral Education.*

Frankenna, William, *Ethics.* Englewood Cliffs, N.J.: Prentice-Hall, 1964.

Kohlberg, Lawrence, "Cognitive-Developmental Approach to Moral Education." *The Humanist*, November-December, 1972.

———, "Cognitive-Developmental Theory and the Practice of Collective Moral Education." In M. Wolins and M. Gottesman (eds.), *Group Care: The Education Path of Youth Aliyah.* New York: Gordon & Breach, 1971.

———, "Continuities and Discontinuities in Childhood and Adult Moral Development Revisisted." In Baltes and Schaie (eds.), *Life-Span Developmental Psychology: Research and Theory.* New York, Academic Press, 1975.

———, "Development of Moral Character and Moral Ideology. *Review of Child Development Research*, Vol. I., pp. 383-427. New York: Russell Sage Foundation, 1964.

———, "Education for Justice. A Modern Statement of the Platonic View." In T. Sizer (ed.), *Moral Education.* Harvard University Press, 1970.

————, "The Moral Atmosphere of the School." In *The Unstudied Curriculum: Its Impact on Children*, Norman Overly (ed.). Washington, D.C.: Association for Supervision and Curriculum Development, 1970.

————, "Moral Development." *International Encyclopedia of Social Science*. New York: Macmillan Free Press, 1968. Briefly summarizes the studies that have been made on morality, articulates the focus of his studies and Piaget's, and summarizes the description of his stages. A good introduction to and survey of the problem—hopefully available in most public libraries, certainly available in college and university libraries.

————, "Moral Religious Education and the Public Schools: A Developmental View." In T. Sizer (ed.), *Religion and Public Education*. Boston: Houghton-Mifflin, 1967.

————, "Moral Development and the New Social Studies," *Social Education: Journal of the National Council for the Social Studies*, May, 1973.

Kohlberg, L. and C. Gilligan, "The Adolescent as a Philosopher: The Discovery of the Self in a Postconventional World." *Daedalus: Journal of the American Academy of Arts and Sciences*, 1971.

Kohlberg, L. and R. Mayer, "Development as the Aim of Education." *Harvard Educational Review*, Vol. 42, No. 4, November, 1972.

Kohlberg, L., P. Scharf, and J. Hickey, "The Justice Structure of the Prison—A Theory and an Intervention." *The Prison Journal*, Autumn-Winter, 1972, Vol. II, No. 2.

Kohlberg, L. and P. Turiel, "Moral Development and Moral Education," in G. Lesser (ed.), *Psychology and Educational Practice*. Scott, Forman, 1971.

Kohlberg, L. and Robert L. Silman. *Preparing School Personnel Relative to Values: A Look at Moral Education in the School*. Washington, D.C.: Eric Clearinghouse on Teacher Education, 1972. Gives some analysis of responses to illustrate application of stage criteria and suggests means available to teachers to raise children's moral levels. Available in libraries with Eric collections and at Regional Resource Centers; Philadelphia area: RISE, 198 Allendale Road, King of Prussia, Pa.

Piaget, Jean, *The Moral Judgment of the Child.* New York: The Free Press, 1965.

Porter, Nancy and Nancy Taylor, *How To Assess the Moral Reasoning of Students.* The Ontario Institute for Studies in Education, 1972. Describes Kohlberg's six stages and how to use the dilemmas to assess the student's moral level. Sample answers are given to clarify distinctions in stages.

Sizer, T. and N. Sizer (eds.), *Moral Education: Five Lectures.* Cambridge: Harvard University Press, 1973.

Notes

CHAPTER I

1. Jean Piaget, *The Moral Judgment of the Child*, p. 122.
2. *Ibid.*, p. 65.
3. *Ibid.*, p. 13.
4. *Ibid.*, p. 111.
5. *Ibid.*, p. 122.
6. *Ibid.*, p. 123.
7. *Ibid.*, p. 148.
8. *Ibid.*, p. 149.
9. *Ibid.*, p. 198.
10. *Ibid.*, p. 251.
11. *Ibid.*, p. 262.
12. *Ibid.*, p. 272.
13. *Ibid.*, p. 280.
14. *Ibid.*, p. 277.
15. *Ibid.*, p. 279.
16. *Ibid.*, pp. 280, 284.
17. *Ibid.*, p. 285.
18. Nancy Porter and Nancy Taylor. *How To Assess the Moral Reasoning of Students*, pp. 37-38.
19. Piaget, *op. cit.*, p. 376.

CHAPTER II

1. L. Kohlberg, "Stages of Moral Development as a Basis for Moral Education," in *Moral Education: Interdisciplinary Approaches*, pp. 86-88 (New York: Newman Press).
2. L. Kohlberg, "Continuities and Discontinuities in Childhood and
3. L. Kohlberg and P. Turiel, *op. cit.*, p. 415.

4. *Ibid.*
5. *Ibid.*
6. *Ibid.*
7. *Ibid.*
8. *Ibid.*
9. L. Kohlberg, *op. cit.*, p. 26.
10. *Ibid.*, p. 24.
11. *Christian Science Monitor*, July 15, 1974, p. 6.
12. L. Kohlberg, *op. cit.*, p. 27.
13. *Ibid.*, pp. 35-36.
14. L. Kohlberg and P. Turiel, *op. cit.*, pp. 415-416.
15. *Ibid.*, p. 416.
16. Martin Luther King, quoted in Kohlberg, "Moral Development and the New Social Studies Lecture," p. 140.
17. L. Kohlberg, *op. cit.*, pp. 53-62.
18. L. Kohlberg, and P. Turiel, *op. cit.*, p. 416.

CHAPTER III

1. William Frankenna, *Ethics*, pp. 5-9, 28-30, 56-59, 113-114.
2. Walter M. Abbott, S.J. (ed.), *The Documents of Vatican II* (America Press, 1966), p. 214.

CHAPTER IV

1. L. Kohlberg, "Cognitive-Developmental Theory and the Practice of Collective Moral Education, p. 353.
2. L. Kohlberg, and P. Turiel, "Moral Development and Moral Education, p. 448.
3. L. Kohlberg, *art. cit.*, p. 368.
4. L. Kohlberg, "Cognitive Developmental Approach to Moral Education," p. 15.
5. Selman, cited in L. Kohlberg and P. Turiel, *art. cit.*, p. 451.
6. *Ibid.*
7. Kreb, cited in Kohlberg, "Cognitive-Developmental Theory and the Practice of Collective Moral Education," p. 346.
8. *Ibid.*

APPENDIX I

1. Piaget, Jean, *The Moral Judgment of the Child.* Reprinted with permission of Macmillan Publishing Co., Inc. First published in 1932.

APPENDIX II

1. These dilemmas are quoted from the appendix of a research report by Marcus Lieberman titled "Estimation of a Moral Judgment Level Using Items Whose Alternatives Form a Graded Scale," ERIC, 1971.